Now for the
good news

GUY

KGUN CLEAR/ACCURIT/TO THE POINT/CUT TO THE CHASE
DON'T STRING ME OUT HERE/ SPILL IT

Now for the good news

by
Guy Atchley

To Marcia,
This just in:
Thanks for all
your help!
Guy Atchley

First edition
ISBN 0-936226-03-X

Printed in the United States of America

Gratitude: I had never felt it so deeply until I wrote this book. Perhaps I had never realized just how much the people in my life had influenced me until their stories stared back at me from the pages you're about to read. These people have blessed my life. I'm confident they will bless yours, too.—Guy

"All lives have magic in them. Some people see that magic and some don't. Guy has not only had magic but magicians, healers, teachers, storytellers, saints and oddballs. He seems to have gleaned something from every one of them. Read this wonderful book of his and you can meet them and learn from them, and as well learn from the ringleader of them all—Guy himself."
John Lee, author of *Growing Yourself Back Up* and *Facing the Fire*

"This is a wonderful, eclectic compilation of stories about many who have faced adversity and personal tragedy and yet still find a way to smile. Atchley relates the stories in a way that each reaches out to us and draws us in, as if we are a part of that particular person's journey. It is so refreshing to share in positive outcomes in a world that is all too often negative. The book made me smile and promise myself to 'whine' less when I am faced with small problems. Thanks, Guy,...well done."
Jim Paxon, Fire and Forestry Consultant, U.S. Forest Service (Ret)

"In a culture where 15 minutes of fame has become just that, Guy Atchley seeks out and retells the small, quiet stories behind the lives of real and honorable people. These anecdotes are sensitive, inspirational and heartwarming. Just the kinds of qualities that make Guy. . . well, Guy!"
Dean Steeves, LaughingStock Comedy Company

"Read Guy Atchley's *Now for the good news* and be inspired! Journalistic integrity, insight and compassion underlie the heartwarming journey of his life."
Amy Weintraub, author of *Yoga for Depression*

"These stories will touch your heart. Guy has been a blessing in our community and expands on that blessing by writing this book. Thank you, Guy, for capturing the adventures for us and sharing both your physical and spiritual search.
Janna Excell, crisis counselor and author of
Soul Light: Connection Between Worlds

"*Now for the good news* is a life-changing perspective on the challenges we all face. Full of warmth and love, these pages may evoke an occasional tear brought on by the reality of human suffering and the realization we have the power to 'be greater than anything that can happen to us.'"
Dennis Carver, photojournalist

To my mother,
Irene Emma Atchley,
in honor of her courage, sacrifice and
undying love for her family

Contents

The Wall

Brief Encounters

The Power of One

Do not assume that he who seeks to comfort you now lives untroubled among the simple and quiet words that sometimes do you good. His life may also have much sadness and difficulty, that remains far beyond yours. Were it otherwise, he would never have been able to find these words.

—Rainer Maria Rilke

Earlene

Leo Rosten wrote: "The purpose of life is not just 'to be happy.' The purpose of life is to matter, to count, to stand up for something, to have it make some difference you lived at all." I want to tell you about the person who made that difference in my life, a person who undoubtedly suffered many forms of discrimination simply because of the way she looked. But, if it were not for this person, I wouldn't have dreamed my dreams. I wouldn't be a newscaster. I would have given up.

You should have heard my first radio newscast at the University of Tulsa radio station in 1969. Unfortunately, you couldn't have heard it. I still remember the song that was playing when the disc jockey pointed at me to read, "Aquarius" by The Fifth Dimension. As they faded out, so did I. I opened my mouth and hyperventilated. Not a single word came out. Mic fright.

I went home that night with the intention of dropping out of college and giving up on my dream of being a newscaster. But instead, I heard these words, "Guy, look at me. Don't you think I've ever felt like giving up? But I didn't. And, Guy, if I can do it—I know you can do it." To understand the force of those words, you have to know about the person who spoke them.

In 1983, I stood in a hospital room in Tulsa and listened to a doctor say, "Earlene, in my medical opinion, you will not be with us by Christmas time. I would suggest you get your things in order. I'm sorry."

Then he walked out.

Standing by Earlene's bedside, I didn't know what to say, but she did.

"He doesn't know me very well, does he?"

Indeed, he didn't. That doctor was not there some forty-five years before when other doctors had given Earlene another grim prognosis. She was two years old when polio attacked her body. Her parents took her to Children's Medical Center in Tulsa where doctors said the family could only wait to see how badly Earlene's body would be crippled.

If Earlene could have stood straight, she would have been about four feet six inches tall. Scoliosis shortened her to four feet two. Long, black, carefully placed hair concealed a hump on her back, and a metal brace made it possible for her to walk ever so slowly. She was chronically ill most of her life. Several bouts of pneumonia in childhood led to congestive heart failure as an adult. Yet, despite the doctor's dire prediction in 1983, Earlene lived nine more years—and she made them good years.

In the final weeks Earlene could not walk. An oxygen tank helped her breathe. I had moved to Tucson, but we kept in touch by phone several times a week. When I would tell Earlene about my petty problems which seemed to be overwhelming at times, she would always put things into perspective for me.

"Guy, if I can do it, you can do it."

On July 19th, 1992, a Sunday, I received another phone call from Oklahoma. This time Earlene was not at the other end. Instead, it was the voice of my cousin, Donna, who had been such a friend to Earlene.

"Guy, we think you should get back here as soon as you can," she said. I caught the next flight. Relatives told Earlene I was on the way. She could answer only with a weak grunt.

I arrived at Earlene's bedside just after midnight, sat down, said the things that needed to be said, and one minute later— she was gone. I will always believe this was her final act of love for her brother. To allow me the privilege of holding her hand, kissing her cheek, and calling her name one more time.

I can tell you this experience changed me. I didn't know how at first. Now I believe I do. I have a new understanding about the brevity of life and how it should be spent—helping others.

I once asked Earlene where she got the strength to go on. This is how she answered:

"I was 22 years old and terribly depressed. All of the other young people were making plans for their futures, and I was wondering if I would even have a future. I had just made Mom-and-Dad's bed, and I sat down to rest. When I leaned back, my elbow came into contact with something. I looked down. There was nothing on top of the patchwork quilt, and there was nothing below it. I felt further. There was something inside one of the patches. Well, my curiosity got the best of me. I got some scissors, cut the patch open, and reached inside."

The following is an excerpt from Earlene's diary, December 11th, 1956:

Dear Me,
I was making Mom-and-Dad's bed this morning when I found sewn into the quilt a little silver cross on a gold chain. I still wonder where it came from. Gosh, it just looks like a sign of encouragement at a time when I need it the most. I put the cross on. I can only hope it will keep up my morale.

Love,
Me

Before Earlene died, she gave me that little cross. It remains my most valued possession.

I share this story not to convert anyone. Different people have different answers to the questions of life. This was Earlene's answer. Mine are quite different. I do share this story because it's all about the power of one, the power to be greater than anything that can happen to you.

The most common way that people lose their power is by believing they have none in the first place. Many times in my life I've wondered what I could possibly do to help others. I've known the heartbreak of being laughed at, the feeling of failure after being fired from a couple of jobs, and the despair of shame—the feeling that, for one reason or another, you just don't quite measure up, in my case literally. Still, through it all, there's always been a fire burning deep inside me, a fire placed there by a tiny woman who convinced me I do have something to give this world—even if it is only words.

Karl Menninger wrote: "The central purpose of each life should be to dilute some of the misery in the world."

Each one of us has that chance today: To give a sign of hope at a time when someone needs it the most. To send that all-important message: I acknowledge your pain. I've felt pain myself. But I made it through. And if I can do it—I know you can do it. *This is the power of one.*

Buried Treasure

Kim Fisher and his father discovered one of the great treasures of the world. They knew that in 1622 a Spanish galleon had sunk off the coast of Florida in a hurricane. They knew it was loaded with gold and silver, but nobody knew where it was. Kim Fisher and his father decided to look for it. They looked for five years; people called them stupid. They looked for ten years; people called them idiots. They looked for fifteen years; people called them crazy.

After seventeen years of searching hundreds of miles of ocean bottom, they finally found the treasure—$500 million worth of gold, silver and emeralds. Suddenly, people were no longer calling them crazy. They wanted to be their friends. In fact, they wanted to share the wealth. Both the state of Florida and the federal government filed lawsuits claiming part of the treasure should be theirs. The case went to the U.S. Supreme Court. And guess what? The court ruled—finders keepers.

We, too, are going in search of a treasure. This treasure is called *The Power of One*. It is buried deep inside you. You are the only one who will ever be able to find it. If you don't, it will be the world's loss. The search will not be easy. It may take years. Other people will try to discourage you. They'll criticize you and laugh at you. At times you'll feel like giving up. But if you persevere, you'll find your treasure. And when you do—it's finders keepers.

My sister Earlene as a young girl

Earlene with our sister Jo who still lives in Oologah, Oklahoma and likes her privacy.

My sister Earlene remains my guiding light.

Enjoying the excitement of Christmas with Dad

Waiting for Howdy Doody on Saturday morning, I would watch the test pattern.

The Backyard Baseball Gang I'm in the back row with my friend Dennis (right). My niece and two nephews, Tony, Dindy, and Juny, are in front.

I wanted to be Superman. I turned out to be Clark Kent.

My first appearance on TV in Tulsa, Oklahoma. The Big Bill & Oomagog Children's Show in 1959. I'd won a bicycle for drawing a stagecoach.

9

Even though decades separated these photos, my father never seemed to age.

Mom was a looker in her polka-dot dress.

Mom taking tickets at the old Criterion Theater in Sapulpa. The show must have been "Ain't Misbehavin." That's what it says on her little hat.

Mom put me through college by working as a department store salesperson. I could never begin to repay her.

11

My first radio job was at KMOD FM in Tulsa. On the air we said "K-Mod"— off the air we called it "commode."

At work at KRAV FM in Tulsa, where we played beautiful music all the time

I had just been in TV a short time when a news photographer snapped this shot of me while I was covering a conference.

Winning my first speech contest.
Sapulpa High School, 1967

After all these years, I still love to make
people laugh.

My best buddies from school days in Sapulpa, Oklahoma. L to R: Vic Fitzgaireld,
retired biology teacher in Alaska; Dennis Napier, retired petroleum engineer in
Edmond, Oklahoma; Don Scott, a truck driver who still calls Sapulpa home. And me.
Dennis probably summed it up best: "I thought I was coming to see my friends, not
their fathers."

Dad: The Things I Remember

I can still see him in that easy chair, the same one he'd had for half a century. It was like his throne, and as far I was concerned, he was the king.

As a child I would play in the sandbox at the edge of our house. Dad would pull into the driveway in his battered, green panel truck. He'd step out wearing white, paint-spattered overalls, his face red from the sun that reflected off the house he'd been painting latex white.

He'd ruffle my hair with that big hand, and say, "Hello, boy." The smell of paint thinner followed him into the house. I'd follow, too. I always knew it was payday when he'd bring home a six-pack of Schlitz and a pack of El Producto cigars. It was his gift to himself after a hard job.

For supplies Dad would often make trips to Oklahoma Tire and Supply. I loved to go along, especially on hot summer days. Oklahoma Tire was air-conditioned, and the cool linoleum felt good to my feet. Oklahoma Tire had the unmistakable smell of rubber. But if you went down the right aisle, there was also the smell of leather—baseball glove leather. I'd had my eye on a Wilson glove for months, and it was still there. I'll never forget the day Dad said, "You want it? It's yours." He seemed pleased to be able to get it for me.

Dad was about forty when Mom took his picture in the back yard. He was wearing a straw hat, kneeling, leaning over on one knee, and grinning. That black and white eight-by-ten photo still hangs on the wall in Mom's house. It was one of the smartest things I ever did when I had Dad strike the same pose in the same place for a new color photo thirty years later. Aside from a

14

few more wrinkles and the disappearance of his mustache, Dad looked the same to me.

One of my most vivid memories of Dad was when a salesman came to our door. From the next room all I could hear was Dad trying to convince the man not to be afraid of our dog, Tammy. She liked to chase people, but she never bit them. It didn't work. Her growl was too ominous. The next thing I knew Dad was on his knees gasping for breath. At first I thought he was hurt, but then I could see he was trying to catch his breath because he was laughing so hard. I looked out the window and witnessed what prompted his reaction. Our dog was chasing the salesman down the street. She was literally on his heels as the man zigzagged down the road until they disappeared around the corner. That was the hardest I ever saw my father laugh.

One of the saddest days came when I had spent the night at my sister Jo's house. The doorbell rang, and there was Dad. He started crying, trying to say something, but the words wouldn't come. Finally, all he could say was, "Brownie's dead." My little dog had been killed in an accident. We'd kept him on a leash in the back yard. He jumped over a chair and hanged himself. I don't remember much after Dad broke the news, just the warmth of his arms and the dampness where his shirt soaked up my tears. I suppose that was the first real pain from loss I had experienced. It would not be the last time Dad and I cried together.

Many years later I remember the phone call from a thousand miles away. It was Dad asking, "Would you pray for me today?" It was followed by another question, "Why is this happening?"

I spent what time I could with Dad. In the end he wanted me to return to work while he fought the cancer. I remember our last goodbye, the feeling of the stubble on his face, his trembling arms that once had been so strong. I later sent him these words:

> It's amazing what we have
>   In this thing called a mind,
> And if we search there long enough
>   There are treasures we can find,

15

Love, peace, contentment and joy,
And somewhere in your memories, Dad,
You'll find a little boy.
He loves you as much as he ever did
In our times of laughter and tears
And that feeling has grown only stronger
As we've aged through the years.
I don't know what to say
When you ask me the question "Why."
I only know that I love you, Dad.
And I always will.
Your son,
Guy

I must have been about seven years old. Uncle Fuzzy, Dad's brother, paid us a visit from California. It was a hot day in August, and the family was sitting around in Grandma Atchley's living room. I was sleepy and worn out from the excitement of having my favorite uncle with us. I crawled up on the sofa and lay down as the family sat around me talking. I remember the voices, the gentle breeze coming in through the window, and the feeling that I was surrounded by love, totally at peace. This is the feeling I go back to time and again when I think of Dad. And these are the things I remember.

Cancer claimed the life of Earl Atchley on February 11, 1990. He was seventy-nine.

Mom

She's ninety now, but still young. She'd be working if she could—that's just the way she is. My earliest memories of Mom at work go back to the old Criterion Theater in Sapulpa, Oklahoma. I have a picture of her wearing a little paper hat as she sold tickets. The hat bore the name of the movie, *Ain't Misbehavin'*.

When times got tough, Mom looked for a better-paying job in downtown Tulsa. She applied at Holly's department store, and they hired her on the spot. I loved riding in Dad's old panel truck to pick her up. I'd never seen buildings so big. On the ride back home, Mom would always laugh when I pointed at the Arkansas River and said, "Big Muh." She still reminds me of this every time we cross the river.

Mom was a saleslady, and she was good at what she did. They made her a manager in the women's lingerie department. And then other stores wanted her. She worked at Dillard's department store many years before she retired.

Mom worked for decades, all the while taking care of family needs. She'd often stay up all night tending to my sister Earlene whose body had been weakened by polio. Then Mom would make breakfast, go to work all day, and come home to fix dinner. Her stamina was remarkable, and her fried potatoes were to die for.

It was Mom's hard work that allowed me to go to college and reach my goal of being a newscaster. She still loves to watch my newscasts when I send her tapes. And if you were to visit Mom's house, you'd see what our family affectionately refers to as "The

Guy Atchley Museum." It seems as though she has every picture I've ever taken, and they're all hanging in her living room.

I remember going back to Oklahoma a few years ago to file a story on my hometown of Sapulpa. Photographer Jon Perra was with me, and the tape was rolling as I knocked on Mom's door to surprise her. When she opened the door, I've never seen anyone quite so flabbergasted. She threw her arms around me, and said, "Oh, Guy." Then she looked at Jon, his camera still rolling, and said, "Hello, whoever you are."

When we went inside Mom's house, her Christmas decorations were still up in mid-January. She's always loved Christmas. When I was a little boy, she'd put a 33 rpm record on the hi-fi and we'd wake up on Christmas morning to the sounds of jingle bells and stacks of presents under the tree.

Of course, Mom had a way of making every season magical. I must have been about six years old when she took me to the Tulsa State Fair for the first time. It was nighttime and the giant Ferris wheel glowed in the dark. As far as I was concerned this was Disneyland. When we rode the Ferris wheel to the top, the chilly autumn air took my breath, and mom held my hand a little tighter.

I also remember noticing Mom's hand in church one day. I discovered the index finger on her left hand was stiff. I asked why. She smiled and told me about the time she was cutting tall grass with a sickle and she made a mistake. She almost lost the finger, but she was thankful just to have it—stiff or not.

I guess that's the secret to Mom's smile. She's always chosen to focus on what she has left—and to be thankful for it.

When I was a teenager working at Sears in Tulsa and Mom was working down the street at Dillard's, we would often ride back to Sapulpa together. And on the nights when the skies were clear, she would always point to Venus and say, "That's our star. It's shining just for us tonight."

Mom has always had two words for everyone she meets—God bless. Well, Venus is still in the sky. Mom is still a dreamer. And, yes, the people who know her certainly have been blessed—especially her son.

Aunt Nellie

Aunt Nellie. I love that name and all it means to me. A gentle soul with a knowing smile and a cackle for a laugh. She called me "Hun" and "Darlin'" and said, "I luv yew" so convincingly.

One of my earliest memories of this woman who lived one block down the street came on New Year's Eve. For some strange reason at the stroke of midnight my mother would stand on the edge of our porch waving a flashlight, and Aunt Nellie would stand at the corner of her yard ringing a cow bell. These sisters would be yelling "poth." I had no idea what that meant.

I felt better some years later when I learned they didn't know either. It was just something they said when they celebrated.

These sisters went way back. Irene was first on the scene in 1914. Little sissy Nellie happened along in 1921. Two little girls who loved to play shopping. Nellie would make her purchase. Irene would say "That be 95."

Nellie and my mom, Irene, grew up on Third Street. They both married men who lived on Second Street, and that's where they all settled for the rest of their lives.

When I learned that Aunt Nellie at the age of eighty-one had passed away, the tears rolled down my cheeks. I felt profound loss and undying gratitude for what she had given me.

Sometimes it takes a while for us to realize what we have in our lives. I finally began waking up in my forties. It was then I discovered the treasure of Aunt Nellie.

Anytime I went back to Oklahoma I was drawn to her back yard. Just to be around her was to feel at peace—especially in her garden, surrounded by roses and robins and bluebirds. Aunt Nellie opened my eyes to the beauty of nature and the truth of the old saying "Happiness is to be found only in your own back yard." To this day I trace my love of birds and flowers back to her garden. She helped me see the miraculous in the ordinary. But the most beautiful thing in Aunt Nellie's garden was Aunt Nellie herself.

At her funeral I looked around and realized that if people wanted a testimony for her life, they need only look at her four children, six grandchildren, and six great-grandchildren. They were her best work. They are her legacy of love.

Aunt Nellie taught us to live simply, feel deeply, and give freely. She warmed out hearts, brightened our days, and inspired us just to be kind to one another. She loved good gospel music, a hot cup of coffee, and pictures of old barns.

She lived a simple life and a noble one. She never preached a sermon. She didn't have to. Her life was one. This was my Aunt Nellie.

Lonnie

The year was 1958. It was a sweltering summer day in the dusty little town of Sapulpa, Oklahoma. I didn't know it, but someone was about to change my life forever. A rather rotund man with a flattop haircut ambled down the sidewalk. When he knocked on our door, my sister answered. We had never seen this man before, but there was something about him that you liked, even before he said a word.

"Hello, my name is Lonnie Campbell," he said with an Okie accent and a smile. "I'm the preacher at Forest Hills Church. We just wanted to invite you down this Sunday."

Invitation accepted. I was nine years old when I first met this man everybody called "Brother Lonnie." Sunday after Sunday I would listen to his words of love and encouragement, but it would be many years before I would understand the profound impact of his words and his actions on my life.

Over the years I watched as Lonnie ministered to our family. He baptized my sister in her own bathtub because her polio-stricken legs would not carry her up the church baptistery stairs. He comforted our family on the days when my grand-mother and uncle died. And when I graduated from high school Lonnie called me in front of the congregation to say how proud he was. I also remember the tears that streamed down the face of this former U.S. Marine as he pleaded with parishioners to love one another.

I entered college, and Lonnie went to another church to serve in a different capacity. Only once did I take time out of my busy schedule to write to the man to tell him just how much he meant to me, but at least I did do it once.

Years passed and there was another knock at my door. My mother's voice was shaking as she held up a newspaper and said, "Guy, there's an article in the paper about a man who died today." It was Lonnie. He had suffered a heart attack after working in his flower garden.

Later, as I wept with the many others whose lives Lonnie had touched, my mind went back to his many acts of kindness. Whether it was his coat for a shivering homeless person, a basket of food for a needy family, or just some words of encouragement for someone in need of hope, Lonnie was always there. His greatest joy in life was telling the old, old story about a cross on a hill far away. And because of him, I can tell my son the story of how his middle name came to be—Lonnie.

A Tribute to Tom Foley

Tom Foley was a big man. He stood more than six feet tall with a bushy beard that made him look like Paul Bunyan. His shoulders were broad and strong enough to carry a heavy load, but he spoke softly with a West Virginia accent that he never lost. And when Tom wrapped his arms around you, it was like being hugged by a lovable old bear.

Tom Foley was a builder. He built houses, schools, and churches. He also built a good life based on hard work and devotion to family—his wife, Rosetta, and their children: Jenny, Shad, and Amber. Tom once told me that he knew in his heart he would always love his wife. And he did.

Just a few weeks before Tom left us, he hosted a cookout in his back yard for the extended family. You could always see Tom because he towered above the rest. As he stood over the grill preparing the food he talked about the house he had built for his daughter, Jenny, and the house he planned to build for his son, Shad.

At this and every meal came Tom's inevitable question, "Who's going to ask the blessing?" Most of the time it was Tom who would bow his head and say, "Dear Lord, we thank you for this day, and we pray that you would bless this food to the nourishment of our bodies. Amen." Despite his health problems Tom was thankful for what he had. And, based on the things that matter most in this life, he was a very rich man.

When the mourners gathered at the Freewill Baptist Church in Sapulpa, Oklahoma to say goodbye to Tom, it was difficult to find a single person who had not benefited from his generosity. I'm one of those people, a brother-in-law whom he treated like a brother. For Tom there was no such thing as an unimportant day and no such thing as an unimportant act of kindness. Much of the time the kindness came in the form of labor. Tom would show up with his hammer, his ladder, or his tractor, and quietly go about doing whatever needed to be done.

Tom Foley's life was a blessing. He blessed us with his work and his words and his presence. His was a life lived well. It was patterned after the life of another carpenter, one who promised to prepare a place for him.

And so, after more than half a century of hard work, Tom Foley was laid to rest—this man who embodied faith, hope and love. This is what Tom Foley stood for, and this is why he will be missed. Yes, Tom Foley was a very big man.

The Journalist Formerly Known as Shrimp

The Journalist Formerly Known as Shrimp

For me it began the first day of first grade. I walked into the classroom and quickly found out my name was no longer Guy Atchley. It was shorty, dwarf, runt, midget, shrimp, little Guy. Kids don't mince words.

The second grade brought a whole new set of names when poor eyesight resulted in a thick pair of black horn-rimmed glasses. I became Mr. Peepers, four-eyes, coke bottles, bullet-proof glasses.

These names followed me through school until the eleventh grade when I got another surprise. I became "Guy Acne." Within the year my face was pitted and scarred. This did not help my fragile self-image. With my classmates relentlessly making fun of me, I turned into the class clown.

My strategy was simple. I would laugh at myself before they could. All the while on the inside I was crying, and I felt like dying.

Eventually the emotional pain became so severe, I was forced to change. I was going to college by the time I decided contact lenses would be in order. After a quick examination, the first optometrist bluntly said that he could not fit spherical lenses on my cone-shaped eyes. The astigmatism was that bad; I, however, was undeterred.

After getting the same diagnosis from a series of optometrists, I finally found one man in Muskogee, Oklahoma who specialized in low-vision cases.

"Can you help me?" I asked.

"Maybe," he replied.

A dozen pairs of contact lenses later, I had a pair I could wear two hours a day. That was good enough to allow me to be on TV without looking like Woodsy Owl. (Eventually, contact lens technology improved, allowing me to wear soft lenses all day long.)

Next stop: the dermatologist.

"Can you get rid of these scars?" I asked.

To my delight the answer came back, "Yes, I can."

"But," he said,

"But what?" I asked.

"It's going to be painful," he cautioned.

I didn't care how much it hurt. I just wanted something done, and I told him so. The doctor explained that he was talking not so much about physical pain as he was psychological pain. People might stare at me.

"I'm used to that," I said. "Let's do it."

The dermabrasion began with what the doctor called a slushy-icepack treatment. He rubbed my face with a little gauze bag full of dry ice. When he was done, my face was one big scab. It usually took about three weeks for the skin to dry up and fall off. Every time it did, my scars were diminished.

The doctor was right. People stared. Some would ask if I'd been in an accident. I told them it was part of my plan to be on TV someday.

As for my height, I grew—not physically, but mentally. One of my favorite quotes is from Eleanor Roosevelt who said that nobody can make you feel inferior unless you let them.

I'll never forget my first television awards ceremony. The emcee announced, "The award for best general reporting in the state of Oklahoma goes to—Guy Atchley."

The spotlight focused on me, and the crowd applauded as I made my way to the podium. My dream had come true. This was my moment. Then, it happened.

One of my co-workers yelled out, "Hey, Guy, why don't you stand up?"

The applause turned to laughter, my pride faded into embarrassment, and I felt like crawling under the nearest table. It was my moment all right. It certainly was not the way I'd envisioned it, but it was a turning point in my life. For the first time I realized that, like it or not, I probably would hear words like those for the rest my life. And I have. The number one comment from viewers who see me in person is, "You're not as tall as you look on TV." One newspaper even said I should be taken off the air because I "televise too tiny." And a tall female co-anchor once referred to me as her "little anchor action figure."

I can laugh now. In fact, I laugh all the way to the bank with the money I make from speeches punctuated by "short" jokes. The breakthrough came when I learned that I would never be able to control what others said about me. I could only control my reaction.

Abraham Maslow defined a "self-actualized person" as one no longer concerned about the impression he is making. Maslow said a "self-actualized person" listens to the opinions others have of him, but does not let those opinions adversely affect him.

But perhaps M. L. Boren said it best with these words: "Get enough education so that you won't have to look up at anyone. Then get some more education so that you don't look down at anyone either."

"And You Call Yourself a Reporter"

I worked ten years to land an anchor job in my hometown of Tulsa, Oklahoma. It lasted ten months until I was fired. Here's what happened.

I was assigned a story on teenage alcoholism, and I wrote that teen alcoholism had reached epidemic proportions. A photographer informed me that he was using file video of a teenager drinking from a can of beer. It was a stupid mistake on my part. That picture seen at the same time as I said the word alcoholism implied the young man in the file tape was an alcoholic. I failed to check the tape before it aired, and as soon as it did, I knew I was in trouble.

The next morning that teenager reportedly showed up for work only to be fired by his boss who said something about not wanting an alcoholic as an employee.

The next firing would be mine.

The boy's parents called their attorney, the attorney called my news director, and the news director called me. He wanted to see me in his office immediately. The meeting didn't take long because it doesn't take long to say, "You're fired." As I walked out the door of his office, just for good measure, he added the words, "And you call yourself a reporter!"

I've had only one migraine headache in my life, and it began immediately after that. For two days I could not get out of bed because my head was throbbing. Those words—you're fired—played over and over again in my head for the next six weeks. I asked myself how I could have made such an idiotic mistake. How could I have done that to the teenager who lost his job? And how could I have done that to myself? Ironically, I had received the Associated Press award for best general reporting in the state three years in a row. I was so depressed that I didn't even look for a job. I spent the next six weeks taking long walks in the Oklahoma countryside. I was a zombie.

While listening to the radio one day, I heard a commercial about a real-estate seminar. The firing made me consider other avenues of employment, so I went to the seminar. That's where I met Tom Hopkins who had become a real-estate millionaire by the age of twenty-seven.[*] I listened to Tom all day long, and when I informed him of my situation, he spent another hour talking just to me. I remain grateful to this day for the time he spent with me.

I never went into real estate, but I came away with some words that can apply to anyone in any business. Tom calls it his Creed of Champions: I am not judged by the number of times I fail, but by the number of times I succeed. And the number of times I succeed is in direct proportion to the number of times I fail—but keep on trying.

Within two weeks I had a job in Oklahoma City anchoring the morning and noon newscasts at KWTV 9. I signed a three-year contract, but the station had options at the end of each year. In other words, managers had the option of releasing me from my contract at the end of each of those years.

It was the last day of the first year of my contract. I was at my typewriter (we were still using typewriters in 1983), and I was thinking to myself—just a few more minutes and I'll have a job for another year. About that time there was a little tap on my shoulder. I looked around to see the station manager who was smiling.

He said, "Guy, could I see you in my office right after the noon newscast?"

I knew what was about to happen.

He said, "Guy, you've been doing a good job for us, but we've decided to make a change."

The general manager replaced me with his son-in-law.

[*] See the next story for Tom's real estate sales secret.

31

Even I was surprised by my next move. I shook the manager's hand, said thanks, and walked straight back to my desk in the newsroom. I picked up the phone and called KGUN 9 TV in Tucson. A few weeks earlier the news director at KGUN 9 had called to ask whether I'd be interested in working there. I told him I wanted to stay in Oklahoma, but if anything happened, I'd give him a call.

Well, I called and said, "Something's happened."

He responded, "I'm glad you called, because I was going to offer the job to someone else this afternoon."

One other note: The news director who fired me in Tulsa went to another station where he was fired, convicted, and sentenced to prison for embezzling millions of dollars.

I've been in Tucson for two decades now. During this time, the Associated Press and United Press International have honored KGUN 9 as the Best Newscast in Southern Arizona seven times, and I've received two dozen awards for excellence in reporting.

And, yes, I *do* call myself a reporter.

It's not what happens to you; it's how you react to what happens to you.

The Pumpkin Man

Tom Hopkins was making $42 a month trying to sell real estate in California. When he quit college, his father said, "Son, we're always going to love you even though you're not going to amount to anything."

Tom says that was his first motivational speech. He got to thinking and came up with a plan. It was almost Halloween. He rented a flatbed truck and paid a visit to a pumpkin patch where he bought hundreds of pumpkins as an investment in his future. He gave away every one of those pumpkins. He left them on people's doorsteps. And he left something else—his business card. Tom Hopkins became known as The Pumpkin Man. And when somebody needed to sell a house, guess who they thought of?

Mr. Hopkins became a millionaire. Today, he lives in Paradise Valley, Arizona. And what does he say about success? He says "Goals are the key." You've got to know where you're going if you're going to ever get there.

Author's note: I'm forever indebted to Tom for taking time to coach me after I'd been fired from an anchor job in Tulsa in 1982. He was the right man at the right time—and still is.

The Anchor Who Saw the Light

Some reporters will let nothing stop them from telling a story.

In your house a typical light is 100-watts, perhaps 250-watts. In a television studio a typical overhead light is 5000-watts, and many of these lights hang over the heads of anchor people. It's not good to be under one when it explodes. Merrill Linn McKean was.

Merrill Linn was reading a story live on the air when the viewers at home heard a loud pop and saw a bright flash. Merrill Linn jumped and her eyes bugged out, but she kept reading. A split-second later, viewers saw a tiny speck fall into Merrill Linn's perfectly styled hair. No one realized it was a glowing piece of filament—until a few seconds later when tiny puffs of smoke began rising from her head.

Unaware, Merrill Linn kept reading, albeit a little faster and with a certain sense of urgency. Merrill Linn's co-anchors were aware and wondering what to do. Viewers could see hands reach in from each side of the screen frantically trying to fan out the smoldering anchor. There was concern that Merrill Lynn might spontaneously combust.

Just as a cameraman took out a fire extinguisher and prepared to use it, Merrill Linn finished her story and the newscast went to a commercial. They removed the filament, and a slightly smoked anchor was able to relax.

But Merrill Linn could be proud because through it all she kept reading.

Co-anchor Julie Myers dons gloves while working in the chilly newsroom. See "Julie and the Elevator"

Julie Myers preempts Michael Goodrich's Friday night "Whoopee!"

Norma Cancio—"The Girl in the Red Suit"
(below) Norma with her family—
John, Norma, and children:
David, 10, Timothy, 9, Andrew,
6, Joey, 3, and Mark, 3.

Reporter Terry Gonzalez primping before going on camera. Terry makes me laugh.

General Robert Johnston giving his expert commentary during the Iraq War, 2003.

(below) Co-anchor Colleen Bagnall and I grabbed a photo op with Peter Jennings when he came to Phoenix to anchor World News Tonight.

Early News Center 9 Team. Left to right: Robyn Zimmerman (weather), me, Stephanie White (co-anchor), Ed Sorenson (sports). Photo circa 1984.

Colleen Bagnall reporting on the Aspen Fire of 2003. Micah DeLacy is behind the camera.

Meteorologist Paul Huttner points to the smoke from the Aspen Fire.

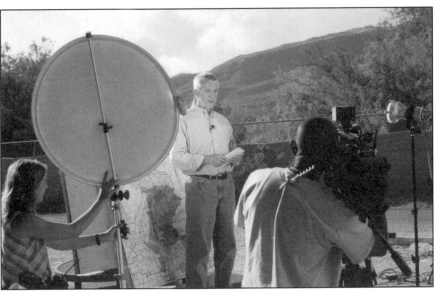

Reporting on the Aspen Fire

Deanne Donnelly in Safford covering the Nuttall Complex Fire on Mt. Graham in July of 2004. Courageous firefighters and a change in weather kept the flames away from cabins and telescopes..

A beaming Maria Neider at the annual Associated Press awards banquet. The AP honored Maria for her reporting on the Aspen Fire. And KGUN 9 News won Best Newscast.

KGUN 9 Reporter Jana Vaughn with a smile of relief in the aftermath of the Rodeo-Chediski Fire in 2002.

Gail Aschenbrenner with President George W. Bush (See Gail's story, "What I Believe," in the Memorable People *Section)*

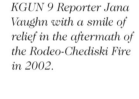

Reporting from Show Low just minutes before the town was evacuated as the Rodeo-Chediski Fire approached, June 2002

KGUN 9 photographer Jim Shields watching as the black clouds of smoke obscured the sun

Tracking the path of the Rodeo-Chediski Fire...

The Pax Man at work

View of the Rodeo-Chediski Fire from Show Low High School—June 2002

When I cut my hair short in June of 2001, I had no idea what a furor it would cause.

The Hair Apparent

The Tucson Weekly once wrote that my hair had not moved since 1957. Well, they can't say that anymore. My life changed on June 21, 2001. "Cut it short," I said. And the stylist did. I was not prepared for what followed. KGUN 9 TV received more than three hundred e-mails, phone calls, and letters.

In my three decades of broadcasting I had never received this kind of response from any news story. Years later people on the street are still stopping me to weigh in on whether they like my hair. This would tend to support Linda Ellerbee's assertion that all the viewers really care about is whether the anchor has changed his hair. Most comments are positive. People say I look ten years younger. Now that I'm in my fifties I appreciate that. However, someone always has a different take.

Vince LaZara asked, "Why did you thank the person who said the hairstyle made you look younger? That seems to imply there is something bad about looking older. I think it is time that society rids itself of the 'youth cult' mentality and accepts aging as a natural phenomenon that does not diminish one's dignity."

Comparisons were inevitable. People said I reminded them of Mr. Peterson on Seinfeld, Joe Isuzu, or Gary Condit.

Weatherman Michael Goodrich slicked back his hair one night and said he wanted to "impress the chicks." One young man told me his mother is now in love with me. My co-anchor Colleen Bagnall says she's jealous because nobody ever made this much fuss over her hair. And the hairstylist who started this whole thing, Veronica at Gadabout, says she's sick of hearing about "Guy Atchley's hair."

Finally, there was the woman who turned on the television, saw my hair, and dropped a wine bottle on her foot. She had to go to the emergency room for stitches. I know this is true because she sent me pictures of her bandaged foot. Fortunately she does not hold this against me. I can only say I'm sorry for the pain and suffering my coiffure has caused.

Dark Days at Inspiration Rock

Arizona saw two of its worst years ever for wildfires in 2002 and 2003. I cancelled my vacation in June of 2002 to cover the Rodeo-Chediski Fire in the White Mountains. In June of 2003 I left for Spain to spend three weeks in a secluded area with no communication. It wasn't until I stepped off the plane in Phoenix at the end of my vacation that I heard someone mention "the fire on Mount Lemmon." I immediately asked what happened. When the person responded that more than three hundred homes and businesses had burned, my heart sank.

When I came back to work the next day, Colleen Bagnall, who had anchored the KGUN 9 coverage of the Aspen Fire, had left for her vacation. Everyone thought the fire was virtually over. We were wrong. Over the Fourth of July weekend, it flared again and I got my turn to cover the flames as they worked their way down the Tucson side of the Catalina Mountains. Fortunately, the fire stopped before causing any more destruction of homes. However, the mountains were charred and changed for generations to come.

After it was all over, I sat down with Colleen to get her take on the Aspen Fire of 2003.

GA: June 17th, what happened?

CB: On the night of June 17th we reported that there was a fire but it wasn't very big at that point. I really didn't think much of it. It was a couple of acres in the Catalina Mountains and not threatening any structures. It was about five to ten acres. Then the next day, the 18th, we went up the mountain to cover it. We stood on Inspiration Rock and watched a huge cloud of smoke.

You couldn't see anything, and we were breathing it all in. The Forest Service kept saying the Type One team was coming and that things were going to change. And I didn't know what that meant.

The A team of firefighters took over at six o'clock that night. I'll never forget at eleven o'clock that night we could see the fire growing before our eyes. There'd be this big flare up and all of a sudden the whole side of the mountain was on fire. At that point we knew it was going to be bad. The Forest Service had about one hundred firefighters on the job at that point.

They told us for safety reasons we had to leave the mountain, but we wanted to spend the night in the live truck and get up in the morning and do the live shots in the morning. And they said no, we are trusting that you will leave because we can't stay out here with you because our shift is up.

GA: *Do you think anybody did stay?*

CB: No. They told us we would never be allowed at a fire scene if we stayed, so we left. I think we were the last ones down. The next morning we had crews go up the mountain, but they had to evacuate.

GA: *The evacuation was on day three?*

CB: On that day I never went up the mountain. At about 12:30, I went on the air from the studio at KGUN 9 to report the evacuation. We didn't have much information.

They had a scout camp and church camp up there and we figured they had about three hundred people, but they were down lower. So, they didn't think there was any danger. But then two dangerous things occurred: The fire went wild and the electricity went out. And they didn't want three hundred kids up there without electricity. So, on the air that's what we focused on because we were inundated with parents calling to ask if we'd heard anything regarding their kids. Meanwhile, the sheriff's department was at the base of the mountain not letting parents up. That's all they needed was to have parents getting lost up there looking for their kids. And at least they knew what kids were accounted for.

GA: *So, on day three everybody was getting out.*

CB: Yes. Up until then, it was a voluntary evacuation for the residents of the mountain. Some of the Summerhaven people told me that they left some of their stuff behind because they thought it would be the same old drill, just like the Bullock Fire. You go back down and you come back up.

GA: *What was your reaction when you heard the fire had gone through Summerhaven?*

CB: Paul Huttner and I were live on the air when a producer told us through the little earpieces that we wear. Paul was talking about the weather and then he said the fire had gone through Summerhaven. We didn't know if that meant the fire had wiped out Summerhaven or whether it had just gone through a small part. We had no idea at that point. Then we got some aerial video from a helicopter, and you could see some of the beautiful homes were on fire. And we knew those homes were just a few of the hundreds on the mountain. Still, it was very smoky, and no one except the firefighters knew how much damage had been done.

GA: *When did you find out?*

CB: We found out through Pima County Supervisor Ray Carroll on Saturday. He went up on Friday and that was day four. I talked to him on Saturday at the Sabino Canyon Fire Command Center. He looked like he had not had any sleep. His eyes were glossed over.

He said, "Colleen, you have no idea what it looks like up there, no one could ever describe what it looks like up there"

I said, "Please try."

He said, "Nothing is up there. Nothing, nothing. nothing."

I asked, "What about the main drag, the businesses?"

"It's all gone," he said.

Ray said he didn't sleep for days after that. He couldn't believe he had to bring this news down. When the area was surveyed later, it was determined that about seventy percent of the structures had actually burned.

GA: *What effect did it have on you?*

CB: When I heard Summerhaven had a lot of damage, my heart started pounding. I felt really bad. I just started talking about all the good memories I have of the mountain. I talked about the last time I was there. My family had gone up for the snowfall, and we had rented a cabin. That cabin was destroyed in the fire. I almost got teary-eyed. When you talk to some of the families, you learn the cabins they lost had been in their families for generations. For each family it wasn't just a home that burned, it was a major part of their lives.

GA: *I think some people would say that Mount Lemmon is the heart of Tucson.*

CB: Yeah. You could drive 30–40 minutes to be in weather 20–30 degrees cooler and the pine trees and all that. I think it is the heart of Tucson.

GA: *How many straight days did you cover the fire either from the studio or from the mountain?*

CB: Eleven days.

GA: *So, it was just about the same number of days I was in the White Mountains for the Rodeo-Chediski Fire. What effect did it have on you?*

CB: It was smoky, of course, and we were all coughing. It was hard to breathe. My lungs were hurting, and we had to wear masks because it was so bad.

GA: *In the midst of all that tragedy, there were a couple of lighthearted moments.*

CB: (Laughs) Yes, we're out in Oracle and we're in these people's back yard and they were so nice to let us use their back yard. We had to jump over this barbwire fence and then stand out in this desert area. This particular day we were very rushed, so I'm already stressed and we walk out there to do a live shot and it's about 3:30 and we're late so they tell us thirty more minutes. I look down and I see all these red ants.

I freak out about red ants because when I was a younger reporter I was too scared to tell a guy that I was standing in an ant hill and they were crawling up my legs and biting me. So, I always think of that and how they were biting me and I was trying to interview this guy and get out of there. I got in the car and took off my pantyhose and shook out all these red ants. The photographer thought it was so funny. I was young, it was probably the third interview I'd done.

So, I see these red ants and I start to freak and stomp on them and everyone is laughing at me 'cause they think I look like a madwoman. The owner of the house said I have something to help you. It was this white powder stuff. I didn't just put a little bit on, I put it around in this huge circle. There's this huge circle around me because I didn't want them getting me. By the end of the day our shoes, socks, and ankles were all white because I had put so much out there. And CNN was laughing because they can see that I'm bending down and they're asking, "What is she doing?" If I hadn't had that stuff I would've been moving around throughout the entire live segments.

GA: And then there was Sal Quijada...

CB: (Laughs) Oh, so on Thursday, day three of the fire, we're on live, we have crews all over. We have Sal Quijada at the base of the mountain interviewing people as they're being evacuated. So, they're coming down the mountain and I have to keep going to him because he's where all the action is. He's interviewing the deputies, and all these people. And then during this live report he coughs as if he was choking on something. Then he cleared his throat and he did it again, and this time it looked like he was going to throw up. So, I thought he was choking. So, I was just staring at him. It looked like he wasn't going to make it.

49

It wasn't until three days later that I actually saw Sal in the newsroom and asked him what happened. He said he was so embarrassed. He had had bridge work on his teeth, and his bridge was only temporary. So he started to swallow it and then he coughed and got it in place but then it slipped again and he nearly swallowed it again. (Laughs) And then, I'm in the manicurist nail shop and one of the clients says, "Yeah, I don't remember what station it was, but there was this one reporter who nearly barfed on the air." (Laughs)

GA: *When you went back up the mountain to cover the return of the property owners, what did the people tell you?*

CB: We will rebuild. They just said that over and over again. One woman came up to me and said, "My home is the A-frame right down there. It didn't burn, and I feel just so bad. I'm not going to go around and flaunt my lovely home. So, don't tell anyone that's my home if you take pictures of it."

We didn't. I think everybody had these strange feelings about everything. And then I met a volunteer with the Red Cross who helps in this area. He said he expected a lot of people to be crying. Instead, he saw a lot of people banding together to help each other.

I'll tell you one thing: It's totally different seeing the pictures and video of the damage and then seeing it in person. You always go around that bend to Summerhaven. Now, it's so abrupt. There's not even a bend anymore. It's just flat and ugly. The weirdest thing was Carter Canyon. Those homes were destroyed. I think there were thirteen or fourteen homes there, and only two survived.

I think the most encouraging thing I heard was from Phil Mac. He owned a general store and cabin, plus he had his home up there. He said when Summerhaven was first built, it was a hodge-podge style. People just built a cabin here and then opened up a cookie store just because they thought it looked nice. Nobody ever worked with anybody else. Now, we have an opportunity to make this very uniform and have a theme. It'll be fun. They can

50

make it in the theme of an Alpine village or something like that. He said it'll be much nicer, newer and they'll try to make it look as rustic as it was before.

Author's note: Just before this book went to press, I learned that Collen Bagnall was leaving KGUN 9 to spend more time with her family. I've never worked with a more professional anchor than Colleen, and I wish her the best.

"When Hell Came to the White Mountains"

That newspaper headline said it all. I first saw the Rodeo-Chediski Fire as I drove out of the Salt River Canyon. The huge black clouds of smoke loomed fifty miles away. I'd never seen anything like it, and I knew it was going to be one of the biggest stories I'd ever covered.

When the KGUN 9 News team arrived in Show Low on that hot June day in 2002, law enforcement authorities let us know we would be part of a grand experiment. For the first time the U.S. Forest Service would allow members of the media to stay in a fire camp alongside the firefighters. But to do so, we had to obey certain rules. Rule number one: we could not leave the camp, which was situated on the campus of the Show Low High School.

What a sight—more than four thousand firefighters pitching their tents on a baseball field. It was tantamount to a new Arizona town with the inhabitants coming from all over the country. As promised, Uncle Sam took care of the media. He gave us sleeping bags and catered food. We even had a laundry service.

We had arrived in Show Low on a Friday. By Saturday the fire was on the edge of town. U.S. Forest Service spokesman Jim Paxon said it was not a question of *whether* the fire would sweep through town, only a matter of *when*. (Fortunately, this prediction proved to be wrong.)

People have asked me if I was scared during this time. Not really. Paxon pointed to the houses across the street from the high school and told me they might burn, but we would be ushered into a building and protected should the fire move through. Surrounded by some four thousand firefighters—no, I never felt scared.

However, I did feel frustrated. Just a few miles away from us hundreds of homes were burning, people's lives were being altered forever, and we could not leave the high school parking lot. This rule led to some heated exchanges between reporters and U.S. Forest Service officials. When a crew from CNN defied the order and went to the fire line, they did manage to file an intriguing report, but they were kicked out of camp the next day.

Even news helicopters had to stay away from the burning areas because of the danger of midair collisions with the air tankers which were difficult to see in the smoky skies. By Saturday evening the converging plumes of smoke near Show Low looked like a giant tornado ready to consume everything in its path. At exactly 7:00 p.m. the order to evacuate came down. We were on the air with a special report one minute later. I stood by a news vehicle, turned up the radio, and held the microphone close to the speaker as the Emergency Alert System went into effect. This was one of the eerie moments in our coverage, because none of us had ever heard the EAS actually utilized before.

Within minutes the roads out of Show Low were bumper to bumper. Most evacuees headed for the Round Valley High School Dome in Eagar. Others fled to the homes of relatives in other parts of the state. Before the evacuation I had asked the owner of Charlie Clark's Steakhouse where he would go. He said, "The next nearest bar."

What to take? Imagine that you have just minutes to grab what is most important in your life. What would that be? In this disaster and in others, researchers have found the one thing most people want to save is their collection of family photos. Many people were forced to make the difficult decision of leaving their pets and livestock behind. We heard stories of how firefighters took time to leave water for thirsty animals. In one case a firefighter offered a hungry dog some tofu from a sack lunch. The dog declined.

As evacuees crowded around TV sets to find out if their homes had been spared, one man loomed large. Jim Paxon, the fire information officer for the U.S. Forest Service, became the calm, reassuring voice delivering the nightly news that would either leave people relieved or confirm their worst fears.

Thanks to a change in weather and the valiant efforts of the firefighters, the flames stopped on the edge of Show Low. The town named after a card game still had luck on its side. The people of Pinetop-Lakeside also knew their towns had been saved. But further to the west, it was a different story. In places such as Timberland Acres, Heber-Overgaard, Clay Springs, Pinedale, and Linden, hundreds of homes disappeared in a wall of flames.

Even so—as bad as it was—it could have been even worse if courageous firefighters had not put their lives on the line to save hundreds of other homes. To this day I get a little choked up when I think about the men and women who did not hesitate to give everything they had to help others. Signs all over the White Mountains thanked the firefighters, law enforcement officers, and volunteers for their sacrifices. And perhaps the sign that said it best was on Charlie Clark's Steakhouse. It read: *Our homes, our lives, our thanks.*

During the Aspen Fire and the Rodeo-Chediski Fire it was my privilege to work with the U.S. Forest Service to provide information. We focused on the people affected by the fires. But what about the people who brought you the stories? They have stories of their own. I asked Jim Paxon to tell us about himself. Here's Jim Paxon—in his words.

The Pax Man—In His Words

by Jim Paxon

I laugh about being born in a sandstorm in Lubbock, Texas (one of the last big black Dust Bowl type sandstorms) in 1947. I was raised by wonderful, caring Christian parents who set a good example for me and have guided me through life. I was my grandad's only close grandson and so I was his shadow until he died when I was thirteen. He was a square-headed Dutch farmer with an infectious laugh like Santa Claus. Poppa Garrett taught me much through the use of homilies, catchy little sayings that "stuck." I've used them ever since. Things like: "There is never a right way to do a wrong thing!" or "Don't ever get in a p—n' match with a skunk, 'cause you'll end up smellin' just like him!" That really refers to getting down on someone's level if they are being mean-spirited, rude or just plain ugly." Another saying was: "Without valleys, there would be no peaks!" That one really got me. If you have ever been through Lubbock and the South Plains, you quickly realize that there are no peaks or valleys. Poppa was talking about the trials and tribulations of life, and it took me another twenty years to begin to realize that he was right, and we should accept the valleys as challenges and growth opportunities. He taught that "the sweetest sound to a person is their own name—pronounced correctly!" There are many others that just come out and I don't even realize that I am using them until it is brought to my attention.

Five young men took a trip to the Pecos Wilderness in 1965, the summer between our Junior and Senior year in high school. District Ranger Charlie Wright imparted wisdom and ethics and "how to's" for most of two hours at the Pecos Ranger Station and we then spent a week in that high mountain forested paradise. Three of us decided that we wanted to be foresters and all three of us went to school in Nacogdoches, Texas at Stephen F. Austin State University and earned degrees in Forest Management. I was the only one of the three that went to work with the U.S. Forest Service.

I went to my first forest fire in the summer of 1969 on the Angelina National Forest south of Lufkin, Texas. It was 400 acres and was considered to be a disaster. After the fire, timber was salvage logged and sent to a sawmill and the area was replanted to pine trees. I have worked in fire ever since and found it to be one of the most satisfying parts of my career. As a bureaucrat, you suffer some frustration from not seeing timely changes in management and results on the landscape. Fire is an adrenaline rush against a worthy foe. You work with great people in a team situation all across the nation and often see folks that you have not seen in years. After the foe is vanquished, you go home the victor to share and revel in the memories later. Sometimes you grieve in the losses of forests and homes and sadly mourn brother or sister firefighters lost in the line of duty. It is truly a family and a system that works due to the highest caliber of professionals.

I retired from the Forest Service in January 2003 after more than thirty-three years of a most blessed career. For example, when Smokey Bear died in 1976, I had the honor of driving him home to Capitan, New Mexico where he was interred in a State Park near the fire where he was burned and rescued from in 1950. I worked at Vail, Colorado when Beaver Creek Ski Area was built and I skied with presidents, Olympic champions, senators and such. I was the District Ranger at Gunnison, Colorado and had a part in the 1984 World Cup ski races at Crested Butte, Colorado. As the Ranger on the Black Range Ranger District of the Gila National Forest, I carried out prescribed burns. In other words, we planned fires to reduce the risk of catastrophic fires. We burned 114,000 acres in ten years without a single fire getting away. The benefits of "good fire" that emulates Mother Nature are so obvious in those lightly burned areas. I have ridden my fine steed, Drummer Boy, in some of God's most magnificent mountains. I spent two-thirds of my career as a district ranger, a ground level decision-maker and manager and lastly, I don't think that I can remember even five or six days in that thirty-three-plus years that I did not want to go to work.

The Rodeo-Chediski Fire was a historic event that caught the attention of the world. With the loss of 470 homes and businesses and 468,000 acres, it was as climactic as a fire gets. I was the Forest Service spokesman. Some people in the media dubbed me the "face of the fire." And reporters told me I was the master of "plain speak." All I did was try to keep the media and the public informed with timely and accurate information in a sensitive way. If it was bad, I told them, but I also shared what the firefighters were doing to battle "the monster." If we had victories, even small ones, those were also shared with the media and the public. I have done the spokesman role on a national fire team since 1989 and have done major fires, such as the Cerro Grande Fire that burned through Los Alamos in May of 2000. I still do not quite understand the notoriety that I gained, but I am appreciative that Arizona has adopted my wife, Debbie, and me as absolute family. That is both humbling and quite an honor. In June 2003, the National Academy of Television Arts and Sciences awarded me a special Emmy for exemplary service to the public in the information operation of the Rodeo-Chediski Fire.

Now I am working with NBC, Channel 12, in Phoenix as a fire commentator and as a consultant for forestry and fire issues. Debbie is often with me and we love traveling and visiting new friends as well as old ones. Life is so good and having my partner and sweetheart with me most of the time is the best part of it. I am truly blessed.

The Girl in the Red Suit

A viewer wrote the following letter to my former co-anchor Norma Cancio when she was expecting her second child.

Dear Norma:

I have watched you on Channel 9 news for a long time for you speak well and you have a nice smile. However, it breaks my heart when I see the change that has taken place in your life in the past two years.

Norma, having one baby after another will make an old woman out of you before your time. I hope you have heard of a thing called "birth control." You can look like the girl in the red suit again with maybe a haircut and a health club membership to take care of toning up your body muscles.

All of these comments I have made come from a heart of love, so please don't take offense.

> Sincerely,
> Your friend,
> Helen

Norma now has five boys—and still looks as cute as ever.

Julie and the Elevator

My five o'clock co-anchor Julie Myers told me about something that happened to her when she was a reporter in Medford, Oregon.

She went to cover a Chamber of Commerce meeting one day. She was loaded down with about fifty pounds of TV equipment. She stepped into the elevator, pressed the number of the floor she wanted, and put down the equipment to rest. The elevator went up and stopped on the floor. Julie picked up the equipment and stood there waiting for the door to open.

She continued to wait until she felt a tap on her shoulder. Julie jumped because she thought she was the only one on the elevator.

She turned around to see a room full of people staring at her. The elevator had opened from the other side.

Whoopee!

Weatherman Michael Goodrich (now retired) would sign off every Friday night newscast by throwing confetti into the air and saying "Whoopee!"

One night Julie Myers grabbed the confetti before Michael could, tossed it into the air, and gave out with her own "Whoopee."

Later, Julie received a note from a viewer who was incensed that Julie would interfere with Michael's Friday night tradition. The writer ended with a warning for Julie to "keep your hands off Michael's whoopee."

Skippy

Television stations often bring in consultants to help anchor people with their makeup. I remember one consultant in particular. He came from Los Angeles, and his name was Skippy. He must have worked on me for two hours using the heaviest pancake makeup I've ever seen, followed by mascara, eyebrow, lipstick, and blush. When Skippy was done, I looked like a tin soldier. Then he did the same thing to my co-anchor, Stephanie White. The station had paid for this, so we felt obligated to go on the air regardless of how bad it looked. Within minutes the phones lit up with people calling to question my sexual orientation.

One caller summed it up quite well. He said Stephanie looked like a hooker, and I looked like her pimp.

Weather...or Not

TV weather people love their computer-generated graphics, and you notice the forecasters always hold a little clicker to change the graphics.

Oklahoma City meteorologist Gary England began his forecast one night by saying, "Let's take a look at that national weather map." Unfortunately, the screen was blank. Gary pressed his little clicker again and repeated, "Let's take a look at that national weather map." Still nothing. The meteorologist stood mute as he pressed his little clicker.

Finally, Gary realized he was holding his garage door opener.

Dear Guy Atchley...

Why I try to find a secluded corner in restaurants:

Dear Guy Atchley,

Are you fulfilling the will of God in your life? Recently my husband and I ran across your path in a local restaurant. You know you try hard not to stare at someone, especially when they are eating their dinner, but God showed me such a heaviness on you. You appeared to have no joy and be spiritually empty. I know you told my husband you had just returned from the Holy Land. Did it stir your heart? Is the Lord number one in your life? He should be! No person or job is so important that it takes us from the presence of the Lord. Time's a-wasting! Yes, there's a smile on your lips, but honestly, I felt loneliness heavy with burdens and the joy of the Lord was nowhere to be felt. The Lord is your provider, not man. Even now as I'm writing, I'm praying for you, "Lord, touch him." Use your gifts and talents for the Lord. He needs you on the front lines as one of his chief warriors, girded up by his word and love. God has a special job for you and only you can do it. Oh, what a penetrating effect you could have on this city. What impact you could make for the glory of God.

Don't let sorrow or disappointment from the past keep you down. God will restore that which the Devil has painfully robbed you of seven times over. The joy of the Lord is your strength. Encircle yourself with strong believers to help uplift you. Make time for God. Do not allow yourself to be sidetracked. I see you as a willow tree swaying with the wind back and forth. Stand straight. Do not allow outsiders to color your thinking. God must be number one in our lives.

In today's world, the word "submit" seems almost dirty, but to us Christians when we submit to God, we are set FREE! Victory over this world is ours!! Jesus is coming back very, very soon. The words of knowledge that are spreading across our nation are saying the angels are placing their lips on the trumpets and Jesus is preparing to rise from his throne for his bridge. JESUS IS COMING! SOON!!

Signed,
A concerned Christian

Author's note: I had the flu.

A Letter to My Boss

Sometimes people don't bother to write me. They write my boss.

Dear General Manager:
Who does that Guy Atchley think he is? I'm getting sick and tired of the faces he makes on the news. For a 60-year-old man he certainly acts like a 12 year old sometimes.

Signed,
Disgusted

Author's note: I was 44 when that was written. I'm now 53, but prefer to think of it as 8 Celsius. I now have a standard response for people who write me nasty letters. I borrow these words from columnist H. L. Mencken who wrote: "To anyone who might send something critical of me, here is my response. I'm sitting here in the smallest room of my house with your letter of criticism before me. Soon, it will be behind me."

Memorable People

Over the years I've interviewed the famous and the not-so-famous. Some of their stories will make you laugh; others could make you cry. But all of them will make you think.

The General

General Robert Johnston is captivating. You may know him for his expert commentary on KGUN 9 during Iraq War in 2003. But now I want you to know more about the man himself, because he never fails to inspire.

Born in Scotland and educated in England, Robert Johnston came to the U.S. at the age of eighteen to become a U.S. citizen and eventually a U.S. Marine. He may have started out as what he calls a grunt, but he became a three-star general serving in such places as Vietnam, Korea, Beirut, the Persian Gulf, and Somalia.

GA: Tell me about Vietnam.

RJ: Two tours. Little did we know we'd be there for eight years. I went twice, but some of my contemporaries went three and four times.

GA: Were you ever wounded?

RJ: No, but a lot of close calls. The North Vietnamese were the masters of building tunnels and trenches. They would dig in, and they were hard to get to. They had plenty of artillery, and their guns could actually out-range ours. I lost more troops from artillery fire than I ever did from rifle rounds. Losing a Marine is always hard to handle. I can remember sitting in a bomb crater on a thirty-day patrol with my company. I'm sitting there, eating chow, and there's a kid sitting probably ten yards away, and a round took his head off. Probably a tank round or rocket-propelled grenade. And there were bits of him all over us. On another occasion an artillery round landed on a truck bed where we were unloading ammunition. Our Corpsman tried to save two Marines on the truck but all he could do was give them morphine to kill the pain before they died. Those kinds of experiences you never forget.

When you find yourself in combat for the first time you worry about whether you're going to be afraid when you get into a firefight. What's the fear factor? I personally do not ever remember being struck by fear, I mean fear where you're trembling. I had to be responsible for leading troops and I had no business being too concerned about my own safety. I scrupulously protected my troops by running my company as skillfully as I was capable of. I truly believed that I was going to make it through every combat operation I was involved in.

The point is, I always felt like it wasn't going to be me. I saw people killed all around me. I had rounds going over my head, and had plenty of close calls. It is not hard to become a bit cavalier about danger. I remember one position in Gio Linh—South Vietnamese forces covered part of the perimeter while my company took the rest. Mine fields all around. And you could hear their artillery rounds go off. You'd hear a pop, pop, pop, pop. And because we'd been there long enough, we knew it was going to be eight seconds before the rounds landed in our perimeter. And, frankly, you'd think to yourself "pop, pop, pop," and you'd walk for about two steps, then you'd jump in a trench line.

Later, at another base called Con Thien, for some reason you couldn't hear the rounds, so when a round came in, you didn't know it was coming. We took more casualties there. A company commander right after me was standing there with his first sergeant, a round landed, and it just took off the top of his body. Cut him in half.

My point? It's a high-risk profession, and you expect that to come with the territory. You just have to deal with danger, and always keep it in a box. I felt like I was able to do that pretty well. I never felt scared.

GA: What else came out of your Vietnam experience?

RJ: What is positive is the camaraderie that comes from a situation where you are truly dependent on each other for your survival and success. During the Vietnam period, we had serious racial problems, a polarization of our society, very much black and white. But when you got into combat, it didn't matter whether you were black, Hispanic, or Caucasian. There was no color distinction in my company. Everyone was Marine Corps green. That's the one thing I will always bring back from my Vietnam experience—the quality of the young troops.

GA: You also were in Beirut.

RJ: As a battalion commander I had occupied the building where 242 U.S. Marines died in the bombing of 1983. I had gone back to Camp Lejeune to become a regimental commander and was rotating troops to Beirut for the peacekeeping mission. I had slept in the very cot in the room that the battalion commander was blown out of. He survived, but he's a paraplegic now. I knew every one of the seventeen officers who died and all their wives and many of the senior enlisted Marines. It was a traumatic and life-altering experience for my wife Sandra and me, and it was an introduction to terrorism. It affected the way I approached every combat experience from then on.

For example, when I was sent to the Persian Gulf in 1990, we had an enormous concentration of troops in Riyadh. One of the biggest problems was having thousands of troops in high-rise hotels. I did my own reconnaissance, and because I was so aware of how vulnerable buildings can be, I'd go down and look at every structure. We had Marines in one building twelve stories high, and there was a basement. Where do you think a car bomber would go? Of course the Marines had barricaded one side of it, because it was a one way street. But do you think a terrorist cares if it's a one-way street? They had not provided any security in case terrorists came up the wrong way. We changed that quickly. Those were the kinds of things I looked at to establish security.

GA: *The Persian Gulf War of '91.*

RJ: People talk about oil. Yes, oil was probably part of the issue. But it wasn't for me. I went there to liberate Kuwait which had been invaded by Iraq. Some of the atrocities committed by the Iraqi army were sickening. So, it was an easy mission mentally in terms of personal commitment.

I served as the Chief of Staff to General Norman Schwarzkopf. One of the key challenges was to create a coalition. Building an Arab coalition was especially difficult. We joined the Egyptians because we forgave a $7 billion debt. We joined the Syrians through the Saudis. We don't know how much the Saudis paid the Syrians. And then we were joined by some smaller Arab countries.

The outcome of the battle is now history and it was a great success. What stood out once again was the quality of our troops. My son was there as a lieutenant and I visited him and his troops just before the ground war began. It was inspiring to witness the quiet professionalism of eighteen- and nineteen-year-old Marines. Our troops were the best equipped, best trained and best led in the world.

GA: *Later came Somalia.*

RJ: After four years of the country being torn apart by civil war, we went in under a United Nations resolution to establish peace and deliver food to millions of starving Somalis. Everybody in Mogadishu had a damn gun. Our job was to disarm all the factions so we could begin humanitarian operations.

When we first arrived, countless hundreds of Somalis were starving to death everyday. Within sixty days the death rate had dropped to only a few each day, and those were primarily caused by disease that most often accompanies famine. That too was a priceless experience —seeing what our troops could do to get gunmen off the streets and save thousands of women and children from certain death.

GA: *Of course, you say Somalia, and people think of Blackhawk Down.*

RJ: That happened several months after the U.S.-led coalition that I was in command of had turned the operation over to the United Nations. When we first went in, even though it was under a U.N. resolution, it was a U.S.- led operation and I was in total control. After five months, I was replaced by a Turkish general who reported to the United Nations. After we put an end to the humanitarian crisis, their job was nation-building. Unfortunately, they didn't listen to us.

The United Nations does business differently and it changed everything. We warned them not to try to create a democratic form of government that would meet our model but to let the Somalis decide what they could live with. They're tribal and nomadic, and they do things differently. But almost immediately, the U.N. put a price on the head of the key warlord, Aideed. When I was there, we had talked to him everyday. We didn't shut down his radio station. Even though it was broadcasting stupid rhetoric, it didn't incite violence, so we let him broadcast. We had our own radio station to counter negative reporting of events. Almost the day we left, the Pakistanis tried to close the radio station. They were ambushed. Sixteen were killed and horribly mutilated. This was three months before Blackhawk Down.

Overnight, the U.N. peacekeeping forces became the enemy. Blackhawk Down occurred in October. Eighteen U.S. Rangers and Special Forces soldiers died that day. The Somalis were waiting to ambush them. The U.S. soldiers were the kind of elite troops that will not leave their dead and wounded behind. They went back into the killing zone. It says a lot for the quality of the troops, but that, in fact, resulted in more casualties.

GA: *You've seen so much death.*

RJ: Yes. It has reinforced the values of family and friends. After the bombing in Beirut, my wife and I went to every home. I went to more funerals in two months than I have in my entire life. I went to every funeral I could. I realize how my profession affects military families and that while deployed Marines miss their families, it is the families of Marines who put up with the greatest hardships of separations. It's given me a greater appreciation of the importance of family.

I think I'm a kinder person for having been a Marine. I'm more thoughtful of others. I try to find ways to be a positive influence in other people's lives. Life begins to have greater value when you've seen the impact of people losing loved ones. I've seen a lot of it. Plus, you better appreciate how mortal we are.

I survived prostate cancer, and that was a life-altering event for me and Sandra. I was sixty at the time. So, I have a special feeling about the importance of research to find cures for the many diseases that prematurely claim so many lives. I was on the Board of Directors for the Muscular Dystrophy Association. I now am much involved with the Arizona Cancer Center.

GA: Talk to me about patriotism.

RJ: It's a powerful force. Most Americans embrace it. I did it more tangibly in uniform by representing our country for thirty-five years all over the world. I felt every time we went somewhere, we made the place better for it. That's why I have trouble with those who protest our involvement in Iraq.

To see that American flag gives you a warm feeling. I get the same feeling when I hear the U.S. Marines Hymn. It's like the national anthem. I am so proud to have been a Marine, because I know that every place we've been, we've done something good— from the halls of Montezuma to the shores of Tripoli. I've never seen Americans go anywhere with anything other than honest motives to do what is good. And despite the anti-American rhetoric that we hear so much about, it's been my experience that most of the world respects America and Americans.

Our flag counts for a lot, and it's not hard to be patriotic when you believe that what we're doing is the right thing and that we're making the world a better place. But patriotism is not just going to war and waving the flag. It's being respectful of laws, respectful of others. It's how you contribute to make America a better place and to make life better for the people around you. Everybody can make America a better place.

GA: *I think of the slogan: Be all that you can be.*

RJ: Most people don't know what they're capable of doing, either intellectually or physically. Most people don't even know what they can do physically because they've never pushed themselves. People need to push the limits of who they are. See how tough you really are.

Some of the things I did as a Marine people wouldn't even think about. Twenty-five miles in eight hours with a full pack, weapons and ammunition. Running three miles in less than eighteen minutes, followed by twenty pull-ups and eighty sit-ups in two minutes. You might say you can't do that, but I say you'll never know unless you try. Push physically and mentally.

After surviving prostate cancer and getting a pacemaker, I'm down to three miles a day at age sixty-five. But I still push. You've got to know who you are, and you'll never know that unless you push the limits, intellectually and physically. It will make you a better person.

GA: *How has being a Marine changed you?*

RJ: I tend to be much more thoughtful of people, more introspective, always trying to make somebody's day better. If a day goes by and you haven't done something to make somebody feel better, it's not been a good day. It can be a pat on the back, a compliment, or just smiling at people. You never ignore someone who comes into your life who needs help. Life is not easy, and if you always want to take the easy way out, then you may have lived a comfortable life, but you won't have made much of a difference to people around you. Making a difference, that's the bottom line. Everybody must find a way to make a positive difference. You try to open the box that you live in, and to the extent that you help others, that is a way of measuring the quality of your life.

The Story of a Survivor

I listened to the woman relate a tragic story which was played over millions of times during World War II. Even though Gabrielle Schneider is in her seventies, she still has nightmares about something that happened to her more than fifty years ago.

Only in recent years has she been able to talk about it. Before she was able to talk about it, the images came out in her paintings—which is interesting because Gabrielle does not consider herself an artist.

There was the cattle train full of people who were treated like animals. Auschwitz: the lines of men and women headed for what they were told would be showers. A smiling man with a thumb pointing left and right, deciding on a whim who would live and who would die. Somebody yelled for Gabrielle to take off her glasses. She did. She threw them away. That is probably what saved her because the Nazis viewed glasses as a sign of weakness.

Gabrielle's mother was not so fortunate. She went immediately to the gas chambers. Gabrielle also lost her father. He died during the death march to Bergen-Belsen. He had had no water for days. Finally, one night, he spent hours scraping the gold out of his teeth. The next morning, he offered this bit of gold to an SS man, hoping to get one drink of water.

The soldier knocked the gold away, and said, "You cursed pig." Moments later, Gabrielle's father died of thirst. Before it was all over, Gabrielle also lost her two sisters and her brother.

To this day she limps because of that long walk she took to Bergen-Belsen. She walked for weeks in the snow in her bare feet. She can still hear the screams. She can still see the stacks of bones and smell the burning flesh. She can still remember what happens when hate takes control of a country.

Could something like this possibly happen again? We've heard the echoes of Auschwitz in places such as Iraq, Croatia and El Salvador.

One humanitarian agency says that millions of people in this world are still being used as slaves in such places as Asia, Africa, and India. Who is going to change this? I believe the change begins with each one of us. It's only by looking for the good in others that we'll ever be able to find the good in ourselves.

Michael Blake

When Michael Blake walked to the stage to receive his Oscar for writing *Dances with Wolves*, few people had any idea what he had gone through to get to that night of celebration.

If there is one thing Michael has always loved to do, it is write. He decided long ago that, regardless of any difficulties, writing would always be a part of his life. Well, things did get difficult.

For a few years Michael lived out of his car in the streets of Los Angeles, refusing to give up on his dream. But after many years without success, he decided it was time for a change. He traveled to the little mining town of Bisbee, Arizona where he scraped paint off window sills and worked as a dishwasher at the Golden Dragon Restaurant.

At that time, Michael was an angry man, angry at life for always taking from him but never giving anything back. Michael thought he had failed in writing and in life. The lowest point came when he was fired from his job as the dishwasher.

That day he walked up the hill to the end of Brewery Gulch, sat down, and wondered what he was going to do next.

One day later he found out when Kevin Costner called from Los Angeles. He had read Michael's book and wanted to make it into a movie. The rest is motion picture history.

In many ways the triumphant story of U.S. soldier John Dunbar is also the story of Michael Blake. Just when you think all is well, something happens that demands yet another heroic response.

As filming began on *Dances With Wolves*, Michael Blake was diagnosed with Hodgkins Disease. Michael told me that having cancer, in its own peculiar way, had been a blessing for him in that he now takes nothing for granted. When asked what time in history he would like to live, he responded, "Right now, right this minute. I cannot think of a more exciting time to be alive. And believe me—I'm thankful for it."

The Hodgkin's Disease went into remission only to be replaced by a new health challenge, multiple sclerosis. Even so, Michael says he feels good and continues to live life to the fullest.

Michael is now married to a wonderful woman named Marianne. They live on a ranch near Tucson purchased with money from *Dances With Wolves*. Michael and Marianne have three children named after American Indians: Quanah, Monahsetah, and Lozen. And it just so happens that all three of those characters appear as Dances With Wolves' children in the long-awaited sequel *The Holy Road*.

Finally, we'll find out what happens to John Dunbar. You know he'll face many challenges, not unlike the author, who says he writes to inspire. His words are golden, kindled from a life of courage.

During the Aspen Fire and the Rodeo-Chediski Fire it was my privilege to work with the U.S. Forest Service to provide information about the fires. Later, I learned that Gail Aschenbrenner of the US Forest Service had gone through a trial by fire of her own—a conquest of cancer that is a tribute to the strength of the human spirit.

What I Believe

Miracles Happen. Expect Them.

by Gail Aschenbrenner

At age thirty-seven, adventure and opportunity were mine. I had an up-and-coming career with the U.S. Forest Service, a guy I was crazy for, and robust good health. An avid swimmer, camper and hiker, I was rarely inactive except during inclement weather. But an increasingly nasty cough and an uncomfortable heaviness in my chest sidelined me. I saw a doctor at an urgent care facility and left with a diagnosis of bronchitis and prescriptions for antibiotics and cough syrup. It didn't help. On Christmas Eve four weeks later, I was so sick that I posed for holiday photos with my head propped onto my fisted hand because I was too weak to hold up my head. But I smiled and laughed. No one knew how terrible I felt.

Six months later, I was standing in the kitchen, chatting with my boyfriend when I sneezed, spraying the white kitchen floor with a long splatter of bright red blood. My boyfriend, horrified, choked out a plea for me to see a doctor right away. I nodded stupidly, my eyes riveted to the bloody floor.

After weeks of tests, some of which were excruciatingly painful, I was diagnosed with non-Hodgkin's lymphoma, an aggressive but treatable form of cancer that attacks the immune system. The orange-sized tumor in my chest was inoperable due to its placement. My only hope lay in months of aggressive chemotherapy and follow up radiation treatments. A decision not to bank my own bone marrow was an exercise in risk, and thus placed my life in the hands of new treatment regimens that had been shown effective in trials.

My life, once promising, had turned into a nightmare. I was bald. The feeling in my hands and feet were gone, and I wobbled when I walked. My toenails fell out. Food hurt, both going in and coming out. There was no place to hide and nowhere to escape the ravages of the pharmaceutical assault that made me writhe on the floor in pain that only cancer patients understand. In the shower, I bleated tears of agony that provided little relief. At times, I prayed for the strength to live just one more minute, then another, and another. I felt I would go insane during my weaker moments because I could not crawl out of my skin to escape the excruciating physical and emotional pain. In the course of suffering, however, I learned to make pain my friend, and after enduring months of agonizing treatments, I was declared cured.

I was most greatly humbled by the kind gestures of my Forest Service co-workers, distant acquaintances and even total strangers. People I scarcely knew raised money to help offset medical costs, brought food to my house, and took turns taking me to chemotherapy and radiation treatments that exposed them to the dark side of the cancer world. My letter published in Dear Abby prompted people to track me down through letters that were inscribed simply, "Gail Aschenbrenner, Forest Service, Portland, Oregon." At the end of each day, I was sick and fatigued but deeply thankful for the kindness and generosity they gave me when I was at my worst.

The traumatic phase of my cancer experience was over years ago, but it will never be completely "over" for me. During my treatment, recovery and even in the years of post-recovery, my fundamental beliefs were challenged, my faith was shaken, and my trust was broken. But I reformed my tragedy into triumph by accepting and integrating the belief that my "test" was necessary for me to recognize the true nature of my existence and the interrelationship of all things. I can remain detached without sacrificing passion. I can revel in the extraordinary attributes of ordinary things with no apology or explanation to others, as my perspective provides a deeper appreciation than what I had before my cancer experience. Explaining these matters is difficult except to say that suffering brought me closer to God, and my dearest hope is that the price I've paid can be spent in easing someone else's burden.

If All You Have Is Time, You Have Everything.
The Smallest Things are the Biggest Things.
Any Day with Hair is A Good Hair Day.
Good Thoughts Actually Do Count.
Miracles Happen. Expect Them.

Gail is the co-author of *A Visitor's Guide to the Kitt Peak Observatories* by Leslie Sage and Gail Aschenbrenner
Paperback: 80 pages, List Price: $15.00
Publisher: Cambridge University Press; (October 2003)
It is a guide that provides a comprehensive tour of the famous Kitt Peak telescopes and an introduction to the important research accomplished with them. With over twenty optical and radio telescopes, the site reveals to visitors modern astronomy's great diversity. Leslie Sage is a Senior Editor at *Nature* magazine and Research Associate, Department of Astronomy, University of Maryland. Gail Aschenbrenner is a Public Affairs Officer, USDA Forest Service

Kevin Pollak shortly after the Persian Gulf War of 1991

Kevin Pollak after 56 operations

Jerry Lewis in younger, slimmer days

Arthur Dehart IV
melted my heart

My friend David Ralph

My son, Neil, has helped at the Jerry Lewis Telethon many times over the years.

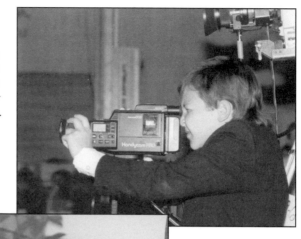

Today he's a first-class videographer and editor.

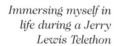

Immersing myself in life during a Jerry Lewis Telethon

Molly Eglin: a real barnraiser

Michael Blake, author of Dances with Wolves, *with KGUN 9 Studio Director Craig Liming, two men who are simply the best at what they do.*

Mary Schaefer surrounded by her artwork with her garden of inspiration just outside the door.

At age 87, Mary Stewart is one of Tucson's top volunteers. She's also my biggest fan and a wonderful friend.

With Leta Kay Kloefkorn, a special friend.

Counselor Vicki Ganon changed my life by suggesting that I — get a life.

These twelve holocaust survivors asked me to give an inspirational talk, but I was the one who was inspired. Gabrielle Schneider is the woman in the center front.

Matthew Barney giving one of those sly looks he was famous for...

Darren Rhodes: A life in balance

Yoga Master Godfrey Devereux lecturing as only he can. "It is always and only — God."

*Interviewing Leo Buscaglia,
"The Love Doctor"*

*Joan Brock:
More Than
Meets the Eye*

Interviewing Mary Higgins Clark

Life on the Edge

You could say that Joan Brock lives life on the edge. Once, she even went over the edge—of a stage—while giving a motivational talk. Joan is blind. And she IS motivational. I talked to her about that time she took flight.

GA: This gives a whole new meaning to "stage fright."

JB: I now have a masking tape that's a fluorescent color. My husband, Jim, thought it was a good way to keep that from happening again. The tape reflects in the shadows in the side of my vision, and it keeps me away from the edge. The tape runs across the front of the stage and up the sides and then a 90-degree angle up the center so that I know where I am in relationship to my stage and my stool.

GA: So, are you blind or visually impaired? And is the word "blind" okay to use?

JB: It is politically correct for me. I was a sighted person who lost her sight. I consider myself blind, but I'm also visually impaired. Technically, if you're blind you can't see anything. Visually impaired means you have some kind of vision, from light perception to tunnel vision to being near-sighted. I come from the philosophy that I'm walking in a hearing/seeing world. If in my journey, I can help people understand about vision loss and blindness, then I've done my job.

GA: How did you lose your sight?

JB: I was teaching at a school for the blind. I'd been there for five years. I was dressing my three year old one morning, looking for her pink socks, and that was the first time I noticed something wrong. The socks looked white. The cones and rods in our eyes give us our vision and depth perception, and the rainbow of colors was starting to disappear. It started with the pink and did not stop. I gradually lost colors, then had a lot of problems with light. So my eyes are very light sensitive. That's why I wear the sunglasses. I still have some peripheral shadows I can see. I have macular degeneration, so I have central loss caused from an autoimmune deficiency that's never really been determined.

GA: *Did you feel sorry for yourself?*

JB: No. Frustrated and angry at times, but I never stayed down in it. I don't consider those moments a depression. I've never stayed down. I just couldn't do that.

I had people comment that I must be saying, "Why me?" But I say—why not me? If I say "why me?" then I'm saying how dare God do something to me. I'm putting myself above everybody else. I'm too good to have something bad happen to me.

My faith has been instrumental in dealing with the loss. I was a minister's daughter. You can't help but go back to certain questions. Who am I? How am I going to get through this? I keep going back to the teachings of my father. I can't tell my story without it.

GA: *Talk about irony. You taught at a school for the blind, and then it happened to you.*

JB: Denial is a wonderful thing, isn't it, Guy? I thought, how can this be happening? I work at a school for the blind. The reality of those moments took some time. And quite honestly, I did not deal with my blindness. I knew how to do it. I dealt with it, but I was buffered by working at the school. I had everything at my fingertips. My husband knew what to do. Everybody in this town of five thousand people were used to seeing blind people. I really didn't deal with my blindness, until my husband, Joe, died. Heavy duty. All of a sudden, it was, oh, I'm going to have to do this. How am I going to pay the bills? How do I get Joy to volleyball? How am I going to do whatever? And that's when I started dealing with loss.

GA: *Tell me about Joe's death.*

JB: Joe's death was so powerful. What I saw him go through with cancer helped me to understand that going blind was nothing. The loss of my sight was a death in my body. It was final. But when you see a healthy, athletic man taken down by such an ugly disease, it was awful. He had cancer of the sinuses. Doctors removed part of the brain, the right eye, and a portion of his mouth. It was awful. His fight lasted seven months. But it was nobody's fault. It just is. You go from here.

GA: *And now, you're remarried.*

JB: When Jim came into our world, Joy was eleven, and I had pretty much given up on dating. I decided I was just going to write in my journal and be a mom. But then I met Jim at a birthday party for a mutual friend of ours. Jim and I hadn't seen each other since high school. He had never been married. We were forty. It was just comfortable immediately. And when he stepped into our lives, he gave Joy her childhood back, because she had been my little assistant. We were forging through life together. Then, when Jim stepped in, we wound up getting married in six months, and that's when I moved to Tucson. It just worked.

GA: *Jim is a writer, too?*

JB: Yes, he's written a book about butterflies. Talk about a metamorphosis. It's quite an analogy for our lives.

GA: *And now, your life is a movie.*

JB: Yes. I wrote my book, *More Than Meets the Eye*, in 1994. In 2002 Lifetime TV sent a scriptwriter to talk to me. And in 2003, it happened—the movie. Carey Lowell plays Joan. Carey was in *Law & Order* for three years as a district attorney, plus she was a James Bond girl in 1989 in *License to Kill*. And, of course, she's Richard Gere's wife. She's beautiful, and she did a wonderful job. But we look nothing alike.

GA: Can you believe all this?

JB: Well, let me put it this way. I'll be at home cleaning the toilet, and I hear my name on TV, and I wonder should I call a friend? What do I do now?

GA: When you deliver your story—whether it's in a speech, or your book, or the movie—what do you hope people take away?

JB: Hope. You have to make the choice to find the hope, pull up your bootstraps, and help each other. We have to help each other. You have no idea how much my friends help me with incredibly kind gestures. Whether it's 9/11, or the war on terror, or the economy, or divorce, or losing a family member to death, or becoming disabled, you could go on and on and on, but we have to find hope. And that hope comes from within ourselves.

The biggest thing that has helped me is thinking I'm helping others by sharing my story. And the most common response I get is—if you can go through that, I need to get a grip. That means a lot to me. But I do share the light side as well.

GA: Speaking of the light side, that might be a good way to wrap things up.

JB: When Joy was nine and we were trying to lead our lives independently—before Jim came into the picture—we were shopping. It was crowded, and Joy was trying to figure out which way to take me. I bumped into someone, and I was going to ask which way the blouses were. I was talking to this person—until Joy pulled me away. She was mortified. I was talking to a mannequin.

More Than Meets The Eye: The Joan Brock Story premiered on the Lifetime channel in June of 2003. It will re-air periodically on Lifetime for a couple of years.

Kevin Pollak

When Kevin Pollak walks down the street, people notice and they wonder what happened. Was it a house fire? Car accident? What?

It was war, the Persian Gulf War. February 27, 1991. The night in Iraq when Kevin Pollak would know pain as he had never known it before. He was driving a Bradley Infantry Fighting Vehicle. It was the middle of the night, the ground war was at its height, and there was confusion in the darkness. Two U.S. tanks opened fire on Kevin's vehicle thinking it was an Iraqi tank. They hit their target with deadly accuracy. Three Americans were killed, four wounded. Kevin's wounds were the worst. His body was badly burned, his face disfigured. His ears were burned off as well as part of his nose and all the fingers on both hands where he'd been holding the steering wheel. He might be blind today if he had not been wearing night-vision goggles.

Kevin underwent a transplant operation. Doctors took the big toe off his right foot and a small toe off his left foot, and transplanted them onto his right hand. So, now, he can pick things up... and with the help of a special device that holds a pen, he can write letters now.

I had not seen Kevin in five years. But then one day I was stopped at a service station and I heard a voice call my name.

When I looked around, I did not recognize the person standing in front of me until he said his name—Kevin Pollak.

He had been through fifty-six operations to minimize the damage to his face. He looked very good, and I told him so.

Despite all that he'd been through, Kevin Pollak looked at me and said, "I've never regretted serving my country—not for one minute." Then he added, "I just love America."

Kevin will soon have a law degree from the University of Arizona, and it should come as no surprise that he will be one of the top graduates in his class. When I asked Kevin what his number one goal would be, his response was simple and to the point. He said, "I just want to help other people like they've helped me."

Without your wounds where would your power be? The very angels themselves cannot persuade the wretched and blundering children of earth as can one human being broken in the wheels of living. In love's service, only the wounded soldiers can serve. —Thornton Wilder

The Judge and the Terrorist

On January 30, 2003, U.S. District Court Judge William Young made the following statement in sentencing Richard Reid (United States vs. Reid) to prison. When the sentencing of the "shoe bomber" came across the wires, I pushed hard to run as much of Judge Young's comments to Richard Reid as we could on our ten o'clock news. We ran only an excerpt, but in this book I can quote it in its entirety. In this post 9/11 world, I believe the judge said what many Americans would love to say to any terrorist.

"Mr. Richard C. Reid, hearken now to the sentence the Court imposes upon you.

On counts 1, 5 and 6 the Court sentences you to life in prison in the custody of the United States Attorney General.

On counts 2, 3, 4 and 7, the Court sentences you to 20 years in prison on each count, the sentence on each count to run consecutive with the other. That's 80 years.

On count 8 the Court sentences you to the mandatory 30 years consecutive to the 80 years just imposed. The Court imposes upon you each of the eight counts a fine of $250,000 for the aggregate fine of $2 million.

The Court accepts the government's recommendation with respect to restitution and orders restitution in the amount of $298.17 to Andre Bousquet and $5,784 to American Airlines.

The Court imposes upon you the $800 special assessment.

The Court imposes upon you five years supervised release simply because the law requires it. But the life sentences are real life sentences so I need go no further.

This is the sentence that is provided for by our statutes. It is a fair and just sentence. It is a righteous sentence. Let me explain this to you.

We are not afraid of any of your terrorist conspirators, Mr. Reid. We are Americans. We have been through the fire before. There is all too much war talk here. And I say that to everyone with the utmost respect. Here in this court, where we deal with individuals as individuals, and care for individuals as individuals, as human beings we reach out for justice, you are not an enemy combatant. You are a terrorist. You are not a soldier in any war. You are a terrorist. To give you that reference, to call you a soldier gives you far too much stature. Whether it is the officers of government who do it or your attorney who does it, or that happens to be your view, you are a terrorist. And we do not negotiate with terrorists. We do not sign documents with terrorists. We hunt them down one by one and bring them to justice.

So war talk is way out of line in this court. You are a big fellow. But you are not that big. You're no warrior. I know warriors. You are a terrorist. A species of criminal guilty of multiple attempted murders.

In a very real sense Trooper Santiago had it right when you first were taken off that plane and into custody and you wondered where the press and where the TV crews were and he said you're no big deal. You're no big deal.

What your counsel, what your able counsel and what the equally able United States attorneys have grappled with and what I have as honestly as I know how tried to grapple with, is why you did something so horrific. What was it that led you here to this courtroom today? I have listened respectfully to what you have to say. And I ask you to search your heart and ask yourself what sort of unfathomable hate led you to do what you are guilty and admit you are guilty of doing. And I have an answer for you. It may not satisfy you. But as I search this entire record it comes as close to understanding as I know. It seems to me you hate the one thing that is most precious. You hate our freedom. Our individual freedom. Our individual freedom to live as we choose, to come and go as we choose, and to believe or not believe as we individually choose.

Here, in this society, the very winds carry freedom. They carry it everywhere from sea to shining sea. It is because we prize individual freedom so much that you are here in this beautiful courtroom. So that everyone can see, truly see that justice is administered fairly, individually, and discretely. It is for freedom's sake that your lawyers are striving so vigorously on your behalf and have filed appeals, will go on in their representation of you before other judges. We are about it.

Because we all know that the way we treat you, Mr. Reid, is the measure of our own liberties. Make no mistake though. It is yet true that we will bear any burden, pay any price, to preserve our freedoms.

Look around this courtroom. Mark it well. The world is not going to long remember what you or I say here. Day after tomorrow it will be forgotten.

But this, however, will long endure. Here in this courtroom and courtrooms all across America, the American people will gather to see that justice, individual justice, justice, not war, individual justice is in fact being done.

The very President of the United States through his officers will have to come into courtrooms and lay out evidence on which specific matters can be judged, and juries of citizens will gather to sit and judge that evidence democratically, to mold and shape and refine our sense of justice.

See that flag Mr. Reid? That's the flag of the United States of America. That flag will fly there long after this is all forgotten. That flag stands for freedom. You know it always will.

Custody Officer. Stand him down."

The Love Doctor

The first time I met Leo Buscaglia I learned why they called him "Dr. Hug." When I stuck out my hand to shake, he pushed my hand away and gave me a bear hug. Leo's books have been a great source of inspiration in my life, and I always jumped at the opportunity to interview him. During one of our sessions, I asked Leo for his definition of love.

LB: Guy, I've studied love for the last twenty-five years, and I'm nowhere near defining it. But I can tell you this. In order to discover love, you have to immerse yourself in life, and then you discover that life itself is love. And in the end you realize the only thing that really matters—the only thing that really counts—is love. So, to me, love is the essence. It is everything.

GA: *You've said before that we learn from our pain.*

LB: Yes, I really do think so. Physical pain though is another matter. I'm more or less talking about psychological pain. Some of the greatest lessons I've learned have come from adversity. It's too bad some people don't want to suffer anything. They want everything to be perfect all the time. Well, life is not like that. There will be tears, and there will also be joy. I tell people embrace the tears, learn from whatever those tears are teaching you, and then go on to bigger and better things. If you're going to embrace anything forever, let it be the joy, and the memories of love and caring, and people and beautiful situations. So physical pain is sometimes very hard to go beyond, but I've seen a lot of people go beyond physical pain, put up with it every day of their lives, and still be cheery and wonderful and positive, and these are the people I think we need to celebrate. We need to thank them because they represent for us—models.

GA: *If it's not too personal, what is the worst pain that Leo Buscaglia has been through?*

LB: Physical or psychological?

GA: *Either.*

LB: Well, you know, I came from a big, passionate Italian family. There were eleven of us, and the thing about having an extended family is that you have to learn very early how to let go and say good-bye. Early in my life I was already experiencing death and learning to cry and learning to feel what loneliness meant. Those are the things that have helped me to understand that the time to live life is now, and the time to appreciate people is when they're alive, and the time to give them the flowers is every day. I've had to say good-bye to everyone from this very large family, and now there are only a couple of us left. I've said good-bye to Mama, I've said good-bye to Papa, and my brother, and those have been the really painful times. There were friends, of course, and relatives. But I think I've made my peace with death, and I think when we understand that we're not here forever, we begin to appreciate the magic and wonder of every single moment, so that I don't want to miss you. I don't want to be distracted. I want to experience everything that life has to give me, and now.

GA: *Speaking of your family, one of your books is about your Papa. What do you want to say about your Papa?*

LB: You know, it was an amazing thing, but people called my attention to the fact that I had spoken so often of my mother who was a big, rotund, happy, lovely woman who loved garlic and loved food and made tons of pasta everyday, but I very seldom had spoken of my father. It occurred to me that this was probably true. My father was more of a laid-back person. He was happy to be in the background. But I thought, when they said this, what a shame because so much of who I am, he was. And I thought maybe it would be nice to let people know something about him, and how he taught us to be caring, loving, beautiful human beings. So I wrote about Papa and it was amazing. Having to deal with all those anecdotes about growing up, and him getting his citizenship papers and teaching us about prejudice and all those wonderful things he did so well, I couldn't help but ask: Did I really take the time to truly know this man? Or was he just a group of little memories, my own memories? Did I ever ask him a question that didn't somehow pertain to me? You know that really shocked me. I wondered whether, in my relationships with other people, am I only concerned with them in terms in how they relate to me? Could I break away from that and see *them* as the most important thing? You know that book made a great difference in my life, and I hope the people who read it, besides having a good time, will pick that message up. Maybe we should start relating to people in ways that don't necessarily relate to us, but are really bent on them, understanding them, seeing them, being curious about their history, that sort of thing.

GA: *I've been in the bookstore before, when people have discovered you've come out with a new book, and they've actually shouted with joy. What's your next project?*

LB: It's going to be a thing that so far is going to be called *Born to Love.* I think it's going to be a kind of bringing together all of these aspects about love that hinder people rather than encourage them to move forward, and then perhaps some ideas about how we can overcome those obstacles, and then be free to love, because I truly believe that all of us are born to love, and I think sometimes along the way, we pick the wrong turn. We become bitter and suspicious, and all that wonderful quality of love that was so beautifully naïve disappears, and then we feel lonely, desperate. We don't need to.

GA: *Do you have a favorite story about love, and how it can make a difference in a person's life?*

LB: Oh, I probably have a thousand, but right at the moment, I think perhaps of one story that has always meant a great deal to me. A young lady in my class at S-C who seemed to have everything in the world; she was beautiful, talented, educated, she could write beautiful things, her homework was always perfect. And one day she just went out and committed suicide. It was the first time anything like that had ever happened in my life, and I think the message of love that came through—and that's a strange thing to say from a suicide—was what does it matter that we teach individuals to read and to write and to spell and to do all of those things that seem to be so important if we never teach them about human dignity? I think from that day forward one of my greatest messages of love was you have to see yourself as a unique human being with a message, with something important to share and to give, then nobody can take that away from you. You do have dignity, you are one of a kind, in a world of many, and I think that is probably one of the loudest and most important messages of love.

GA: *What's your epitaph going to read?*

LB: Oh, that's easy. "Here lies Leo who died living."

Author's note: Leo Buscaglia died June 12, 1998 at the age of seventy-four. His memory and his words of love live on.

Is It Worth Dying For?

Today, when confronted with the prospects of climbing the ladder, more and more people are asking themselves, "Is it worth it?"

In fact, there's a book called *Is It Worth Dying For?* It's written by Dr. Robert Eliot, who explained to me that the book evolved from personal experience. He was the administrator of a new medical center, and he thought the center could not operate without him. He worked seven days a week, fourteen hours a day, until one day his heart began to hurt. It was a major heart attack. That's when he switched roles—from doctor to patient, and he was forced to ask himself "Is it worth dying for?"

His conclusion: "No, it is not."

Most of us spend more time making shopping lists than we do planning our lives. Dr. Eliot says if you want to fight stress, the first thing you must do is clarify your values. How do you do this?

His suggestion is to pretend that you have only six months to live. Make three lists: things you have to do, things you want to do, and things you neither have to do nor want to do. Then, for the rest of your life, forget everything in that third category. You might be surprised at how much time you've spent doing things for no worthwhile reason.

Dr. Eliot almost died from overwork. Today, he lives his life by two rules: *Don't sweat the small stuff* and *It's all small stuff.* Maybe it's time that we redefined the word "success."

Laughter—The Best Medicine

Norman Cousins taught us the importance of laughter in his book *Anatomy of an Illness*. Faced with a life-threatening illness, Cousins prescribed laughter for himself. He watched funny movies in his hospital room.

He found that after a good round of laughter his pain would disappear for a couple of hours. This was a mystery back then, but today, we know the scientific reason why this happened. Endorphins—a painkilling chemical secreted by the brain, our psychopharmacy.

Matthew

It's not unusual when I'm in public for parents to introduce their children to me. They want the kids to meet "the guy from TV." That's how I met Matthew Barney. I pulled out some paper from my journal and drew Bugs Bunny. It's something I do for kids. It seems to impress them. Later, I received a phone call telling me how much it meant to the parents and to Matthew. Just the hour before, he'd been diagnosed with leukemia.

Matthew was born April 9, 1985. To his mother's surprise, Matthew arrived six weeks early, an indication of just how rambunctious this little boy would be. He was always ready for the fun to begin.

Matt despised having his picture taken, but it was something we needed to do to get his family some financial help. He also didn't like to be interviewed, but I tried. Despite my best efforts, Matthew would say almost nothing when the camera rolled, but the instant we turned it off he'd start talking. He'd say things like, "Does your face hurt? Because it's hurting me."

The first time I interviewed Matthew, I was walking across his living room to get a microphone when he stuck out his leg and tripped me. Then he sat smiling as if nothing had happened. Matthew showed his affection in strange ways.

Matthew and his mother made many trips to University Medical Center in Tucson from their modest home in the mining community of San Manuel on the other side of the Catalina Mountains. Along the way they would sometimes see deer. Matthew had heard that if your car accidentally hit a deer, you could keep it. After that, on every trip, Matt carried a deer caller and a knife just in case.

On one trip Matthew succeeded in getting his mother to stop where they had seen two deer on a previous trip. Matthew took out his deer caller and used it. Much to his surprise—and his mother's—a herd of cattle came over the hill.

Matthew's cancer was diagnosed November 25, 1990. How do you tell a five-year-old boy he has cancer? How do you explain it to him? On the way home after the diagnosis, Matthew's father, Shem, noticed a car with a rusty spot. He said, "Matthew, you've got a rusty spot inside, and doctors are going to do all they can to make it go away."

A few days later Matthew informed his father that sometimes people die of cancer. Shem was surprised that his son would know this much about the disease.

Matthew said, "What do you expect? After all, I am in kindergarten, you know."

Chemotherapy left Matthew bald. When he played with his uncle's 45-pound boxer, Pongo, the dog would chase Matt around in the yard and affectionately knock him down on the lawn. Pongo would hold Matt down with one leg across his neck and lick his bald head like a lollipop. Matthew liked this as much as Pongo did.

Matthew never complained about his plight. He tried not to show his pain, but it was there constantly. Matthew stayed with us for ten years, half of which were spent fighting cancer. We tend to measure a life in years, but there is another way—by its impact. Even though Matthew was a little boy, he taught everyone who knew him a lesson in love and strength.

Matthew was strong to the end. Shem and Donna said Matthew sat up on his own and talked in the final moments. When paramedics arrived, they tried to give Matthew some oxygen, but he took off the mask and threw it down. When I heard this, I thought: Wasn't that just like Matthew—to go out just the way he came in—with all the fire he could muster. He did not go quietly—nor should he. After all, he was Matthew Barney.

Just a few hours before Matthew's departure, his father came home from work at 1:30 in the morning, looked in on his son, and was surprised to find him awake.

Matthew said to his father, "I can't sleep because you let all those people in."

Shem was puzzled. He didn't know what Matthew meant. There was no one else in the room. No one that Shem could see.

Arthur

Every year I can count on Labor Day being my most intense weekend. The Jerry Lewis Muscular Dystrophy Telethon never fails to leave me drained, but satisfied that I've done something to help others. I meet countless people, many with the most physically devastating disabilities imaginable.

It was 1985, and I was in the middle of another frenetic telethon. And then for me everything stopped when I turned around and saw him—Arthur Dehart, Arthur Dehart IV. The little boy in the wheelchair was smiling even though he could hardly hold up his head. All I could do was stand there and look at him. My heart was pounding, and I wasn't quite sure why. I felt like crying. For some reason I felt this profound connection to a little boy I'd never met.

A French philosopher once wrote: "There are places in the heart we have not discovered yet; pain must be before we know they are there." In that moment, I discovered those places in my heart.

I never saw Arthur when he was not smiling. I specifically remember a home video of his second birthday. He was wearing a little birthday hat, his wheelchair was pushed up to a picnic table, and his family was singing the happy birthday song. Arthur just smiled as only he could.

Even then, his mother and father knew that Spinal Muscular Atrophy was taking its toll on their son. And, in fact, this turned out to be Arthur's last birthday.

As I prepared this book, I went to get Arthur's picture from his mother, Lani Mitchell. She told me she never knew that I had been so deeply touched by Arthur until she read a comment I'd made about him in a pre-telethon interview a few years ago. She said it was nice to know that her son had left such an impression.

And it wasn't just me, it was many people, including doctors and nurses who had been so affected by him that they felt compelled to write to his mother and tell her so.

His life was short, but it was powerful. I've never forgotten Arthur and what he gave me—empathy. That connection I felt to Arthur has spanned all these years and evolved into heartfelt connections with so many other children and adults who are fighting so courageously against muscular dystrophy.

In the days leading up to each telethon, I take time to visit a little grave at Holy Hope Cemetery. And there among the statues of angels, I pause for just a moment to remember an angel who visited me.

Alex the Dancer

Alex Nowak was a junior at Palo Verde High School when I first met him. Just a few years before, he'd become a quadriplegic in a bicycle accident. Alex's drama teacher had called me because she said I had to meet this young man who wouldn't let anything stop him. Even though his body is confined to a wheelchair, his spirit soars in everything he does.

Alex told me, "You know when I was in the rehab center, I saw other people with problems similar to mine, and I saw how many of them gave up. And that's when I vowed I was going to live a full life regardless of the limitations I may face."

I watched Alex's stellar performance in the school play. I saw the pride of his family and the respect of his classmates. And I know the story we aired must have been a real boost for the people who saw it. Alex's story certainly stayed with me, and it was such a pleasure to receive the following e-mail from Alex a year after our initial interview. He hadn't changed.

"Sorry, it took me this long to send you a letter, but things have been insane. On March 13th I turned eighteen, and to celebrate I went and jumped out of a perfectly good airplane! I went skydiving. I jumped thirteen thousand feet, and had fifty seconds of free fall. The sensation was amazing. And that's not all. On April 10th, I received an award for Outstanding Teen Citizenship. On April 17th, I'll get the J.C. Penney Golden Rule Award. And then, after that, I'm scheduled to receive the Crystal Apple Award. Oh, by the way, I went to the prom with a lovely young lady named Jessica Evans. I've never danced so much in my life. This whole year has gone so fast, and it shows no signs of slowing."

Alex, you're the man. Keep dancing. You certainly make me want to dance.

The Rabbi

It's been said the question in this life is not: Will you experience pain? The only question is: What will you do with your pain? Rabbi Harold Kushner took his pain and wrote a book. He called it When Bad Things Happen to Good People. *The Rabbi writes about the loss of his son who died at the age of fourteen. I asked Rabbi Kushner why he believes his book became an international best seller.*

HK: I think two reasons, Guy. First, it asks a question that sooner or later everybody is going to confront: If there is a God in the world, why do these terrible things happen all the time? Why so much sickness? Why so much death? Why tragedy? Why unemployment? Why bad luck? If you care enough about people, you're going to find yourself asking that question.

The second reason is, when you ask it, you discover that the traditional religious explanations don't help. They're more designed to defend and justify God, less calculated to comfort the grieving person. My book tries to go beyond that and say I'm not interested in the truth about God. I want to make you feel better. I want to give you reasons to hope. I want to convince you that you're not a bad person—and God is on your side.

GA: So, why do bad things happen to good people?

HK: I would have to say that 'why' is the wrong question. "Why" focuses on the past, what should I have done differently, whose fault was it? So I tell people don't ask why, ask when something bad happens to me how do I go on, where do I find the grace and the strength and the desire and the sense of the worthwhileness of life to continue even after the tragedy. And that's where I think God comes in. I don't think God wants people to be sick with cancer and for planes and automobiles to crash. I don't think God wants people to be crippled with multiple sclerosis. When genetics and biology and human cruelty cause these things to happen, I think God wants to give us the incredible resiliency to say even at a time like this, even under these circumstances, life is worthwhile. I am going to cherish life and go on living.

GA: *Tell me about the death of your son and what part that played in the writing of the book.*

HK: My wife and I had a son, Erin, who was born with a very rare condition called Progeria, rapid aging. It speeds up the life process so that very early in the life of the child he stops growing and starts aging and develops all the infirmities of old people when he's still a little boy. It was diagnosed when he was three years old and he died the day after his fourteenth birthday. One of the things about children who know they're going to die is that they're afraid because their life was so short and pain-filled that people will forget them. We promised Erin we would not forget him. There was no way we would ever forget him; he was too much a part of our lives. I wrote the book partly to tell his story and partly to share with others how I was able to cope with this unimaginably bitter experience, how I could go on being a religious person, how I got the strength to go on living.

GA: *What is the key for surviving such a tragedy?*

HK: A lot of people ask me who has an easier time dealing with tragedy. Does it help to be religious? Do younger people have an easier or harder time dealing with it than old people? You know what I found the key is? Self-esteem. If you think you are a good person, you'll pick yourself up, dust yourself off and say that was a lousy break, but that's not going to stop me. On the other hand if you have been taught from childhood by your parents, by your clergy, by your teachers that you're no good, that you deserve to have bad things happen to you, then when it falls in on you, you'll say, "Yeah, that's what my life's always going to be like," and you'll be devastated.

What religion needs to be doing, what friends need to be doing, is giving people the support, the mega-doses of love that will help them feel good about themselves. When we try to make sense of tragedy by saying you must have done something to deserve it, or asking why didn't you do that differently—in the long run you'll see there was a purpose to it—all we're saying to them is: You have no right to feel outraged, you have no right to feel bad. There's probably a good reason why this happened to you. And it's just the absolutely wrong approach.

GA: So how does a person develop self-esteem?

HK: If you chose the right parents (chuckles), if you're lucky in your choice of teachers, the church or synagogue that you grew up in, and some things you have control over: if you have friends who'll be there for you, who don't try to minimalize, but who validate your pain, who'll sit and hold your hand and keep their mouths shut and don't try to explain it, but hug you and sit with you and listen to you. When you get the message that you're worth their time, when your doctor spends time with you instead of sending you off for more tests, when your clergy-man listens to you and holds your hand instead of giving you bad answers, this builds up your self-esteem. When you have the kind of religious view that permits you to feel God cares about what happens to you, not that He's judging you and not that He's meting out punishment because you're not perfect, but that He cherishes you, grieves with you, hurts with you, and is present with you as you try to find the strength to go on because where else are you going to get the strength to go on unless God replenishes it when you use it up? To know that you are important in the sight of God does wonders for your self-esteem.

The question is not the existence of God. The question is: Does God care? If God exists like the South Pole exists, like New Zealand exists, it doesn't make any difference to me. The question is: Does God care about me? The crucial time came when we found out Erin had an incurable disease and that every day of his brief life would be filled with physical and psychological pain. I was terribly overwhelmed by that. I felt I had a bargain with God. I would be a moral person and try to persuade other people to become moral. In exchange, God would bless and protect my family and me. I thought I was keeping my half of the bargain and God had defaulted on his. I lost my faith and I went through a very difficult crisis before I came up with the kind of reconstituted faith that I write about in my books. Understanding what God's role is in helping people cope with tragedy, understanding why, as one of my teachers used to put it, expecting the world to treat you nicely because you're a good person is like expecting the bull not to charge you because you're a vegetarian. The world is not fair, the world is not predictable, the world is not reliable but it's the only world we've got and only through God's help am I able to make it through this world. I came out of that crisis with a more mature, unshakable faith than I had before then. Frankly, I think I would've been happier if that tragedy had never happened, and I still had a childish, naïve view of God because nothing had come along to shake it. I would rather be a very mediocre Rabbi with a twenty-eight year old son rather than be a best-selling author who wrote a book about his son's death.

GA: *What are the most important things you've learned in your life?*

HK: The first most important thing I've learned is that the real human life is the life you share with people. The more you see people as antagonists the lonelier you become. On the other hand—the more you open your life up to include people—the happier, the richer you become. The nicest time in my life is when I know people are dependent on me, and that people will be there when I depend on them. The worst feeling I can imagine is to wake up one morning and know that in the whole world no one could care if I was still there or not. That's why you need to reach out and involve people in your life by caring about them.

The other most important thing I learned is that the childish concept of God and faith that I learned about when I was young—that God is like a super parent who rewards you when you've been good and punishes you when you've been naughty—is wrong. God is a source of love so that when I use up my love and my strength, as the book of Isaiah says, "I turn to God and He renews my strength so I can run and not grow weary, so I can walk and not feel faint."

I now recognize that God does not cause our misfortunes, but he does help us by inspiring other people to help. Let me suggest the bad things which happen to us do not have a meaning when they occur, but we can redeem these tragedies from senselessness by imposing meaning on them. I tell people that suffering leaves you uniquely qualified to help others because you know what's in their hearts. And if you don't help them, nobody else can in quite the same way as you. In the final analysis the question is not: Why do bad things happen to good people? But rather: How do people respond when such things happen?

Denial Ain't a River in Egypt

John Bradshaw is a recovering alcoholic with a message of hope for those who fight addictions. John told me his story when he came to Arizona for a presentation.

JB: I was a child of an alcoholic father. My mom and dad married at seventeen and eighteen. I was born in 1933. I lived with in-laws during the depression, and we moved probably ten times in the first fourteen years.

My dad was just in and out and by the time I was thirteen he was gone. He would be there, and he would be gone; he would be there, and he would be gone. It was very, very confusing. My mother was just a young gal and she did the best she knew how to do. She went to work at a department store and basically it was her raising three kids by herself. It was tough. I had a grandfather and grandmother, her father and mother, who were good to us. And I was a good boy. I was this boy who repressed everything and took care of my mother's pain and took care of everybody's pain around me.

I hit about thirteen or fourteen and I and all the guys from broken homes got together, and we went out and started drinking and soothing all that pain that was inside of us. So I had a pretty wild high school, not breaking the law, except for kids drinking as much as we did. Galveston was in its heyday, the red light districts down there, and it was a terrible way for a kid to have his adolescence, and yet at the same time, I was the president of the class and editor of the paper, a straight "A" student. I always had this super-achiever part, and when I was twenty-one I decided I was going to become a priest. I had this polarity that was always going on, almost degradation or being perfect. You either go one way or the other. You try to be shameless, perfect, righteous or you just give in and become a slob. My life went both ways. I'd be this perfect kid, and then I'd just let it all go.

So I went in the seminary and did that perfect for a few years. I used to kneel for six hours without moving a muscle and just did it perfectly, and then I started drinking about the third year of the seminary and did it all in the closet. I was a very bright kid so they'd look away from my troubles because I was in an order like the Jesuits or the teachers, and I had a very promising career. Finally I just came to the point where I could not go on. I mean the booze got to me, and they got it that I was in big trouble. At that time this religion didn't have any half-way houses so they basically just asked me to leave, and I walked away with two or three hundred dollars to make my way in the world at thirty-one.

It was a terrible time in my life. My drinking increased and by the end of about the thirty-second year I committed myself to Austin State Hospital. I was there for just six days, and I decided I was going into this twelve-step program for alcoholics. That was the beginning—December 11, 1965. That was the day I walked into that state hospital, and I've not had a chemical or drink since then.

That was the turning point in my life and just very slowly people would ask me to talk. I got me a TV show in Houston, a late night talk show that me and another guy did. And then in 1981 I did the family series. I did the eight stages of man on PBS. It really didn't go over that well. Then in 1985 I did *The Family*, and that was the one that opened everything up. In '88 I came out with a book about the family, and I wrote the book on shame, and *Homecoming* spent fifty-four weeks on the *New York Times* bestsellers list. We've sold over two million books since '88.

GA: *What is toxic shame?*

JB: Well, shame is a healthy human emotion. We all need a sense of shame. A sense of shame is blushing. It's being embarrassed when you've made a mistake. It's being shy with strangers. All children of all cultures—this has been studied cross-cultur-ally—have a sense of shame.

Now you move from a sense of shame to being ashamed. The technical way to describe it is that it's become internalized, and it becomes internalized by having your emotions shamed by—What do you feel sad about? People tell you not to be angry. What are you afraid of? Don't get too happy; there are starving children. Your needs get shamed, and all families have some of this. The more dysfunctional the family the more shaming there's going to be.

My mom was twenty-three years old, raising three kids, making a buck and a quarter an hour, she'd come home from work, and here are three needy kids. Well, I got it very early on that if you need around her she's going to be angry. She's going to abandon me. That caused me a lot of problems in my later life especially in my relationships with women—not knowing what I needed, not knowing how to ask for what I needed.

GA: You mentioned the word dysfunctional. How many families are dysfunctional?

JB: My belief is that all families have some dysfunction. Func-tional means you're a human being, and you feel all your feel-ings, and you feel all your needs, and you feel all your wants, and your body works. Now, most of us are raised in a culture that has repressed feelings, especially anger and sexuality. That's how shame gets internalized. Your sexuality gets shamed. Your anger gets shamed. Your needs are shamed. And then suddenly you don't feel shame as an emotion anymore; it's an identity. It becomes a character, and that happens to varying degrees to people, but a functional family, another way to describe a func-tional family, is that it deals; if daddy dies, people grieve, people talk about it. In a dysfunctional family, it will be avoided, it will be swept under the rug. Don't say anything, if you have anything unpleasant to say, go to your room.

GA: *Alcoholism. Same thing?*

JB: Alcoholism is the same thing. Everybody pretends like nothing happened, or the kids buy into daddy sleeps on the porch every night because he has a bad back.

GA: *How depressed did you get when you were drinking? And having felt that low, does that give you a deeper empathy for others going through the same thing?*

JB: Well, I can think of some of the terrible days and those last years of the seminary. I remember a guy who was not a model human being, and I remember trying to borrow two bucks from him for a beer, and he threw it at me. I mean I was a seminarian, studying to be a priest, but I'd been drinking all night, and I found this guy on a street corner. I think of it as a low moment in my life. I was in panic. I needed a drink real bad. In the last days, I was having visual hallucinations. I was bad off, physically bad off with alcohol.

Going through that gave me a sense of compassion, a sense of empathy for other people's sufferings. I know what shame feels like, I know why it's important for me to talk about my stuff, my pain, my foibles, because it helps other people to come out of hiding with theirs, because we need to talk about it. The only way you can heal shame is to embrace it. Its character is to go into hiding. People hide their faces. They want to dig a hole in the ground, and so it's been important for what I do.

Now that I've done my healing work, I realize my dad was perfect. I mean that was just the kind of dad I needed to be where I am now. So I can redeem all that suffering and pain. I can make it, reform it, and see it as what made me—me. It's given me strength. I've been through a lot of bad things, and this is very important because people can get stuck in the pain; they can get stuck in the past. I don't hold my mom and dad responsible for what happened. They were wounded kids themselves, but we've got to understand what happened. The goal of the work is to grieve the pain and to finish the past, so I can be an empowered creator of my future.

118

GA: Tell me about the wounded child.

JB: The wounded child is the shame-based part of us. It's like you have anger when someone shames you. Someone spanks you. They spank you in front of your brothers. Suddenly, that part of you is not okay. Most people have trouble with anger; most people fear anger; most people are manipulated by anger. So suddenly one part of you is not okay. Well, I call the part of you that has been shamed the wounded child. It's the child who goes into hiding, and then you have to develop the good guy, or you have to develop being nice and happy, rather than being angry, so you over-develop one side of your character. Some people are so nice that they don't have any sense of good or evil anymore. They don't have any passion for evil because they're so nice. So the wounded child is the vulnerable part of me. When I embrace my wounded child, it's just a way to package it; it's just a way to say it so that people can understand it.

GA: There's been some research that suggests some people are genetically predisposed to alcoholism and substance abuse.

JB: Well, I have always believed that. I believe that from the first drink, my body didn't metabolize this chemical very well. I had an alcoholic blackout where you have brain amnesia when I was thirteen. It seems to me that is a very powerful chemical signal to a person that somehow you don't metabolize this chemical. So I believe there's a genetic basis for alcoholism. I think there is for certain forms of obesity, for certain forms of sugar disorders.

I like to say that all genetics dispose you to the kinds of the addictions you might have if you've been trained to be an addict. You have to be trained to be an addict. How? By abandonment, by sexual abuse, physical abuse, emotional abuse, by neglect of your development dependency needs, by enmeshment into one of your parent's pain.

I was set up as a child to take care of my mother's pain. I was always watching her. I was always trying to be there to take care of her sadness. Well, I never got to feel my own sadness, and when you grow up in a family where you never get to feel your own feelings—that's the wounded child part of you.

I ran the Palmer Drug Abuse Program in Los Angeles for four years. We never saw what I would call a pharmacologically addicted kid. Every time we did a background of those kids, there was trouble in the family. We'd worked with the parents, and the marriage was in trouble. Those kids had had deprivation, abandonment, abuse, at some level along the way.

Studies are coming out that addiction is like a metaphor of abuse, abandonment, neglect, or enmeshment—where you don't get to have a self, so you have a hole inside you and you're trying to fill it up. That is also why I quit drinking alcohol, and I started working addictively and eating addictively. In our culture we tend to heal addictions with other addictions. We quit smoking, so we start eating. What we've got to heal is addictive-NESS. That's that insatiable part that's empty inside. That's the wounded child. It's very important we heal compulsivity, which is what I call—the hole in the soul. You keep trying to fill it up, but there's never enough alcohol, never enough sex, never enough gambling and excitement, never enough food. So we have to grieve it; we have to finish the past. And that's what a lot of the inner child work is. It's grief work, finishing unfinished business, going back and connecting with the feelings, and grieving it.

GA: *What can people do to help themselves out of addiction? Or perhaps to help someone else out?"*

JB: The worst part of addiction is denial. You're denying that it's really having life-damaging consequences on you. Most addicts know deep down there's something wrong here, and they really want to stop at some level. There was a part of me that always didn't want to do this, but I felt that I didn't know how to escape.

There's wonderful support in every community. You have AA and all kinds of counseling available. Many twelve-step groups are available to people, and they're free. I say to people, just go to six meetings, just go six times, and open yourself to make a commitment. If you have any doubts that you're an addict or not, go and try it, just sit there and listen, and just tell people you're there to listen. You don't have to tell anyone you're an alcoholic. I didn't tell anyone I was an alcoholic in the beginning. I didn't want anyone to think I was an alcoholic. Of course, they'd carried me on a stretcher to the state hospital, but I was an intellectual, and I wasn't like these other people. But as I listened, I thought these guys had been living with me. They were telling my story. And that's what people will say. They go to an overeaters meeting, or they go to a cocaine anonymous meeting. These meetings are free. They're run by people who know the problem, and they're not going to shame you in any way. Then you have treatment centers. There's wonderful treatment available. Sometimes people are in such bad shape they've got to be put in a treatment center. You can do interventions.

Let's say I was the daddy that was the drunk. My two kids, my wife, my best friend, my boss get together with someone that's in AA, say, and I'm just sobering up after a bad drunk. They all walk in my room one morning, and I'm feeling terrible. I've got this hangover. I ate a goldfish last night at somebody's house. I'm feeling embarrassed. And God knows what I've done.

You say, "John, you know I'm your best friend, and remember that day we were supposed to go fishing and you got drunk. I think you've got a serious problem, and I really love you, and there's help." And then your kid says that to you, and your boss says this to you. Bosses can be very powerful. The boss can say to you, "You've got to get help, or we won't keep you on the job. If you get help, you've got your job."

Then this guy says "Hey, I can take you to a meeting this afternoon." Or you might have a therapist. You say I can take you to a treatment center or you have it set up ahead of time. Sometimes addicts feel helpless at the deepest level, so sometimes we have to go in there and help them. One other thing to remember: An addict can't work without a support system, and this is how co-dependency was discovered out of alcoholic work, where it was realized that a spouse of an alcoholic or a drug addict gets as addicted as the addict, but gets addicted to the addict, and the kids all get addicted in the sense that everybody is obsessing on daddy's or mama's or whoever's alcoholism or whatever the addiction is. So if the support system gets the help, and refuses to do that, refuses to cover up anymore, does intervention, that can be very powerful.

Good Golly, Mrs. Molly

Molly Eglin is the founder of the Rincon Valley Farmers Market in Tucson. It was a dream that she made come true. When we met for coffee, I thought our conversation and interview would be limited to the market. Little did I know...

ME: When I was growing up, I was really tall.

GA: *How tall?*

ME: Six feet. I was this tall since the sixth grade. I always felt like a monster.

GA: *So, you got the comments for being tall like I got for being short.*

ME: Right.

GA: *A typical comment would've been?*

ME: Wilt the Stilt, Jolly Green Giant, I was told all my life how klutzy I was. I used to walk completely hunched over.

GA: *For what reason?*

ME: So that I'd be shorter. I had one date in my life before Evan came into my life. No one would go on a date with me. I felt ugly, I felt stupid, I felt dumb. I had no friends. In school I was beat up all the time. I got thrown down a flight of steps once by a gang of kids. I used to go to school and I used to go to the five and dime and buy lipsticks. When the girls would come to push me or whatever I'd be like, "Do you want a lipstick?"

GA: *To keep them from doing it?*

ME: Yeah. I decided I was funny, so I went with it. Anything somebody said I'd try to come back with a quip. When high school came, my behavior became sarcastic. I think what happened is that all the stuff I had in my childhood—being knocked down—has probably given me the compassion that I have today for the people in my life. I understand people. I feel a lot. And I'm able to easily jump into someone's space wherever that may be, because I feel it so deeply. Every Halloween my mother would always put a sash around me and a crown and make me go around the neighborhood dressed up as Miss America.

GA: *Because?*

ME: She felt in her mind that by me going out like that, then that would make me feel better about myself.

GA: *And what did it do?*

ME: It made me feel so unworthy of everything. And that struggle has taken me to this today.

GA: *And today is what?*

ME: Well, today is about realizing that everything I have, everything that I am is what is the most important thing for me. It's about knowing me and being who I am, and staying true to my heart. Being a little bit of something for everybody wasn't working. And being a lot for less is what's working for me now.

In the old days if I was in pain I would run and go and shop. Anything that would happen I would leave. It didn't matter because I didn't have anything inside of me. I couldn't even think of what it would be like to go quiet, to sit quietly in pain. And now when something happens in my life, I go quiet, and feel whatever that pain is. And I know that staying quiet within myself the light will come and I will move to the next place. And that's where the journey has taken me. It's amazing.

GA: *Was there a particular turning point in your life?*

ME: The first one for me was somebody wanting to marry me. Evan. You know, somebody accepting me and loving me—unconditionally—and being okay with whatever I was. But I look back and we were so disconnected. It's amazing that we even made it to today.

124

GA: *Disconnected from everything? So, you loved one another but you were disconnected.*

ME: I was eighteen. That's when I got married. Without my struggles, I wouldn't even *be* who I am today. I would never see life the way I do today. So, all the stuff that's caused me the most pain, I embrace it in a way that embeds my soul. I need to hold on to that. If I were to make it into a bad thing I would never be able to go forward. I would never be able to be the mother I am today.

GA: *Tell me about your children.*

ME: I have two daughters, 23 and 25, Jennifer and Stephanie. They are my light. They say to me that where I was even five years ago is totally different today. The kind of mom I was is totally different today.

GA: *You ran a flower shop for a while.*

ME: The name of my business was Good Golly, Mrs. Molly! No matter what anyone bought I would undercharge. For me to sell someone else stuff was easy, but for me to sell myself was hard. I could never include my labor and my time.

GA: *So what happened because of that?*

ME: I had to close it down because I didn't charge enough. (laughs)

GA: *And after that you ran a modeling agency.*

ME: I was around twenty-nine. I was the receptionist at a modeling agency and then an agent left and I became an agent. It just fell into my lap. I remember getting cards for the first time that said "Molly Eglin, Agent." I will never forget that feeling.

GA: *You helped cast movies?*

ME: Yeah, I brought my talent to casting directors and they would take my people and be in movies. Evan was in two movies. *Desert Bloom* with Jon Voight and *My Science Project*. It was easy for me to push my people and to talk about how great *they* were, but not myself.

I've learned so much about egos, that's why I left. Everything was about "out here" not "in here." It was my life, but I left. It taught me about my ego. It was all about my ego.

GA: *Correct me if I'm wrong but maybe your time at the model-ing agency was all about trying to complete yourself?*

ME: Absolutely. Absolutely. It was like, "Wow, really beautiful people like me."

GA: *Was there any one thing that prompted your decision to leave?*

ME: I was watching how the parents would push their kids. I watched a father yell right in front of me at his seven-year-old son because he didn't read a script right. It freaked me out.

GA: *If you could say something to parents about pushing their kids, what would it be?*

ME: Think about whether they're doing it for themselves or for their children. Most of the parents I met at the agency were living vicariously through their children. And for me that's one of the greatest injustices. It becomes about your dreams and your unfulfillment and your fantasies and your living them through your children. I couldn't do it and I left.

GA: *What next?*

ME: My greatest gift that came into my life was Canyon Ranch. That was my spiritual beginning. That was the beginning of my becoming. I went and applied for this job and they hired me right away. I've always been told I'm so good with people. They just *loved me*.

I applied in the hiking department. It changed my life. I've always been afraid of heights, but I found myself hiking high into the mountains. My fears dissipated. It brought spirituality into my life. I was taking people into the depths of mountains with their fears of being out of their environment. The more I gave them, like telling them to go slowly, watch out for snakes, the more I got out of it. The more I did that, the more I felt whole. The more I started to become. By giving of my heart, the more I understood me. Walking and talking and being at one with someone, whoever that was. Being able to make the greatest connections, friendships. It became a way of being.

Occasionally when I fell, they saw my vulnerability. They saw it was okay to fall. We're human. I would take people on hikes, and while we went high, we'd also go deep into conversations. We'd get done with our walk and they'd either be crying or laughing hysterically.

GA: So, the hiking opened your spiritual connection.

ME: The more I hiked, the more it became a meditative journey. Listening to my footsteps, talking with people, the sounds, the wind, the birds, climbing, walking through my fears brought another way of living.

GA: A healthier way of living...

ME: One day on a hike I got so light-headed, I got so ill. I didn't want to tell anybody so they wouldn't think, "Oh Molly's always sick. Molly can't come into work because she's always sick." I got back to the hiking office and called my heart doctor and drove over there.

When I got there he did a thorough checkup and he said, "Molly, we're taking you off your medication. What you're doing physically has lowered your blood pressure. It's lowering it too much so I'm taking you off your medication."

GA: And you thought...

ME: It was a wonderful thing. The next day I'm at Canyon Ranch and I'm not on my medicine. Who's walking toward me? None other than the founder of Canyon Ranch.

I ran over and said, "Mr. Zuckerman, I have heart problems, and I was on medication but thanks to your hiking department it's lowered my blood pressure and I no longer need my medication and your wonderful Canyon Ranch has given me a new beginning and a new start on a healthy life. Thank you so much."

And he was like, "Who *is* this woman?" Anyway, thank God for Canyon Ranch.

GA: *But you left to pursue a dream.*

ME: I started the barn thing. I still hike and I still go to Canyon Ranch, I just don't work for them right now.

GA: *You moved to the Rincon Valley.*

ME: From my house I started seeing the barn. I went to Evan and said, "I want that barn." And he said, "Molly, we came out here to simplify our lives, we are not buying a barn." And I said, "They're gonna give it to me." And he said, "Who's gonna give it to you?"

And I said, "I don't know, but they're going to give it to me because I want to make a farmers' market." Evan was like, "What do YOU know about farmers' markets?" I said, "Evan it's calling me."

So, of course I don't listen to him and I make a few calls and I found out who owns the barn and it's Donald Diamond. So I handwrite a letter about my vision, about what I want, to do something for the community, because I love this area.

To make a long story short, they gave me the barn. We started with eight vendors and it's now around sixty vendors. We offer everything from produce, salsa, anything for the community, I've given thousands of dollars to the Vail School District. I don't question anything. I knew it was meant to be.

GA: *And you'll be out there for as long as the spirit moves?*

ME: Yep, exactly.

The Counselor

I first met Vicki Gannon when I went into group counseling to help someone else. That's when I found out I was the one who needed help. Vicki held up a mirror and helped me see myself for the first time in my adult life. She helped me see my workaholism, my denial, my faults, and, yes, my qualities. Then she had the audacity to suggest I "get a life."

GA: When you work with people, what's the first thing you do to help them?

VG: I think it's important to know what they want. You'd think just walking into a counselor's office everyone just wants the same thing—to be happy. But within being happy there's so much room. You have to figure out what they want and really truly be there for them, even if you don't agree with what they want. If their goal is to make a million dollars, that's the funny thing. Their negative, materialistic plans may change during the course of therapy. I don't even have to point out any social and spiritual values. It's just their own process of working with what they've got. They realize, hey, this isn't so important, but this person or idea in my life is. That's one of the most exciting things that happen to people. They become centered.

GA: Do you see yourself as a catalyst for change?

VG: Sometimes I don't think I do anything. I just go uh-huh, and yeah, and oh, really? I'm thinking about somebody I'm working with right now. This is a miracle person. I've worked with her only about eight times, and she's gone from the deepest, darkest despair to somebody who's really looking at her values and is excited about herself and everyone around her. I don't take credit for that in any way. I just witness the transformation. I sit there in awe.

GA: *It's kind of like blocked energy?*

VG: Exactly! It is. I work a lot with what you're feeling in your body right now. "Where do you feel that? Is that tight? Is it loose?" And it's great to measure someone's progress with it.

GA: *I was a workaholic. Do you see a lot of that?*

VG: Yes, I do. It has a lot to do with the society we live in. You have a good job, you're attractive, you have a home, a family. I think from the outside you begin to believe that image and go along with what others think about you when in reality that's not all you are. Guy, you learned balance.

GA: *When someone is holding a lot of anger, what do you do?*

VG: I do a lot of expressive work.

GA: *Expressive—meaning?*

VG: Meaning to externalize the anger, like hitting a block or shredding a telephone book, or strengthening your voice.

GA: *Some people might think that's stupid.*

VG: Well, it is—but it works. When you're working with anger it's really uncomfortable because it's contained. People can do expressive work, and it dissipates easier. Anger is good. Anger keeps things alive and kicking. It gives you new references and growth. I encourage anger in couples, expressed appropriately. It's a good energy when it's harnessed.

GA: *What about honesty, being honest with ourselves?*

VG: If you grow up with critical parents, then you learn to be critical. You internalize whatever your parents and your environment have taught you. We are huge self-abusers. We take over right where our parents left off, and we criticize ourselves. We live in this state of image creation. If this is how others see me then this is what I'll be. In reality there's somebody trying to break loose and figure out who they are.

130

GA: *The primary addictions would be drugs, alcohol, food, sex, workaholism.*

VG : Yes. You can turn anything into an addiction.

GA: *Wayne Dyer says many people suffer from an addiction called "more."*

VG: Oh yes. Bigger, better, more. I think that evidence now is really in that a big part of chemical addiction is genetically transmitted. Brain transitions occur when someone uses controlled substances which would account for the craving. So, there's that to look at and you have to work with it. Another thing is that this has probably filled a void for some people, it's a way of coping. Whether it's not feeling good about yourself, or chronic pain, you have to realize that it serves a function. For example, people have turned to drugs and alcohol instead of killing themselves. But then it turns against you and you may end up killing yourself anyway.

GA: *What causes people to change?*

VG: Some people are so self-negating that I think they have to start off with, "Oh, I'm hurting my mother or sister or whomever." And that's fine. It's just an entry point. Then when people start changing, they start truly seeing themselves and they start to become self-motivated.

GA: *But in some cases other people have to intervene?*

VG: Yes. Intervention happens a lot to get people into treatment centers. Interventions are small, little kinds of strategies. Someone with an eating disorder we put a mirror in front of them. They can't look.

GA: *Really?*

VG: Most of them.

GA: *Why's that?*

VG: For people who are anorexic, we do body-tracing. We have them just look down at a piece of paper and trace an outline of what they think their body is. Then you have them lie down and

I trace around them. And then you compare what they think they look like and what they really do look like. It's amazing that anorexic people see themselves sometimes twice as large as the actual configuration. A runner will draw feet that are really long but not much above the waist. Somebody who's been sexually abused, they'll just blank out the whole genital area. This is a start. It gives you a beginning map. At the end of treatment it's so exciting because they see themselves totally differently. I think this is a great goal for most therapy.

GA: *Talk to me about your son. What happened to him, and what part has that played in your life and your helping others?*

VG: Well, I have to take you back a little bit. In all honesty, I was really dysfunctional in my marriage. I didn't do right by my kids. I don't mean I beat or starved them, but I was just emotionally not present. I was constantly in my head some place else. I know now I was trying to cope with chronic depression. I used to have a fantasy about being a bush pilot in Australia and delivering human organs. So, when my kid would talk to me, I was flying a plane to Australia in my head. Anyway, my kids grew up with a father who was excellent, but he was working and they were stuck with me. I don't want to paint a totally negative picture of me. I have learned to see I had some good qualities as a mom. I'm still learning as I watch my daughter bringing up her boys. She is patient and present.

My kids growing up had the usual teenage problems. We're talking about the '70s so there was a lot of drug use and promiscuity. My oldest son got into LSD. Then divorce, and Michael felt considerable pressure being the oldest. My son was one of the few people—approximately ten percent—who use LSD on a regular basis and become schizophrenic. He'd hear voices. We had him in and out of psychiatric hospitals. His father and I knew the dangers of suicide. He had had two previous suicide attempts. We got him therapy, but his third attempt was successful. He jumped off a radio tower at the end of Alvernon Way and wasn't found for eight days.

GA: He climbed up the tower?

VG: Yes, he climbed up and jumped. Of course everyone in our family felt guilt and shame. We all thought we were to blame for Michael's death. But I knew I really was the one to blame. And it's been a long, hard struggle to appropriately be responsible for what I did and didn't do. I was already a therapist when Michael died. I was in another county assessing whether people were a danger to themselves or others and initiating the commitment procedure. I was doing that, and my son committed suicide. It was shattering for me. But in hindsight I was in denial then. Not about Michael, but about how much I was into an image and not really connecting on a heart level with what was going on, still "in Australia."

I tried for a while to work with parents of schizophrenic kids. I had some connection with them but it just didn't feel right. I worked in another treatment center and had some experience with schizophrenic patients, but that hit too close to home. So, I had more therapy myself. Grief and loss seem to be a good compromise for me—to work with people who have suffered loss, even with people who have lost sons. Once I worked with a woman who lost three sons! Little by little she put her life back together. She had a strong spiritual sense that they really weren't gone, that she could communicate with them, and that helped a lot. Yes, it's impacted me a great deal. It's increased my sensitivity to what others go through and allows me to model hope.

GA: How long did it take you to heal?

VG: Michael died in 1978. I got better by paying more attention to my surviving children, and getting therapy. I started to hike and run, and I quit smoking. I got much more of a spiritual consciousness. Michael was into saving the whales and he had hiked all the trails. I think it started off as sort of a link with him but grew into my own passion. I've hiked in Peru, Alaska, and Hawaii.

GA: *So, in a sense you were carrying on what he would've done?*

VG: Yes, people do that with loss. They do things which they feel link them to the deceased. And sometimes they don't even know they're doing it.

GA: *What's in your future?*

VG: My littlest grandchildren. I want more time with them. I want to do more traveling, be more creative around my house, and be more with people. And read more. Books are my addiction, but I don't always remember what I read (laughs).

GA: *We've covered a lot. Anything you'd like to add?*

VG: I just want to tell you how much I respect you, all the work you've done. You entered into enormous emotional pain and reconstructed yourself.

GA: *There's still work to be done.*

VG: Yes, there always is, but celebrate the distance you've climbed. It's a journey, not a destination.

Vicki Gannon has been working in the field of behavioral health since 1973. She currently works at Sierra Tucson as well as maintaining a private practice.

For many years my attitude toward anger poisoned my life. I pretended the anger wasn't there. I thought I was above getting angry. I considered it a weakness of people with no self control, no discipline, or people who weren't nice. I was a nice guy. At least that was the face I wore. All the while I was burning up inside, angry at myself for not being a good enough husband, not being a good enough father, not being a good enough person. With nowhere else to go, my anger turned inward leading to years of depression. Enter John Lee. He taught me to face the fire, and it was a turning point in my life. The following is an excerpt from John's book *Facing the Fire: Experiencing and Expressing Anger Appropriately.*

Facing the Fire
by John Lee

Parent-child relationships are special. Adults can choose whom they relate to—and don't relate to—when they decide this is in their best interest. Children cannot make these choices: They do not choose their parents and must try to grow into emotional self-sufficiency (which many people never do) before they are free from the need to relate to or rebel against their parents.

Further, adults can avoid criticizing other people and their behavior (though in fact few people do). Parents can avoid criticizing their children—and should—but are expected to comment on their children's behavior—and should—because they, as parents, are responsible for teaching their children what is acceptable and appropriate, and what isn't.

Thanks to our culture's misguided values and poisonous parenting methods, being a child is misery for most children much of the time. Though we adults like to pretend this isn't true, most of us know in our hearts that it is. We remember. We can never forget.

Being a child is hard, and being a parent is no picnic either. I know a man who fought in the infantry in World War II, killed enemy soldiers in close combat, saw his buddies killed and badly

135

wounded, and went five months without a bath. He says nothing in his life has been as difficult as having a 14-year-old son.

This chapter discusses how to be angry with your child, how to help your child be angry, and how to make amends to your child for mistakes you have made, whether from anger or some other cause.

IF YOU ARE ANGRY WITH YOUR CHILD

First, be careful. Being inappropriately angry with someone else may hurt him or her. Being inappropriately angry with your child, especially while the child is young, can devastate him or her. It can ruin his or her life. Estimates are that more than 60% of all depressives, 80% of all prisoners, and 90% of all suicides had parents who were inappropriately angry or inappropriately intimate with them.

If you are angry with your child, take big breaths, in and out. Feel what you're feeling, and if it's so strong that it will hurt your child, get away fast and express the feeling in a safe way, by yourself.

Second, do as psychologist Haim Ginott said: Be angry at what your child has done, but never at the child himself or herself.

If your four-year-old daughter throws food on the floor, don't curse a blue streak and scream, "Bad girl!" But don't coo, "What a little piglet!" either, because this would mislead your daughter into thinking you liked what she did, thought it was a cute way to gain attention. Ginott would say that a parent shouldn't criticize or praise a child, only what the child has done. The child's self should always be loved and accepted and never be up for discussion.

Say something like, "Food isn't for throwing, Vanessa. You know that. We throw balls, not food. Come help me clean it up."

If your seventeen-year-old son leaves the car a mess, don't curse a blue streak and scream "You pig!" Instead, say something like, "There's a lot of your stuff in the car, Jason. I'm using the car in an hour, and I count on you to have it picked up by then. "

Third, remember your priorities. A clean car counts, but a lot less than Jason. It would be nice if Vanessa didn't toss food on the floor, but her being secure about your love and her right to be a child and childish without suffering terrible retribution is much more important.

An eight-year-old is playing horsey in the living room and accidentally knocks a vase off a table. The vase breaks. In many American homes, that child is punished—shamed, spanked, sent to bed without dinner. What does the punishment show the child?

"I can be punished for anything, even if I didn't mean to do it."

What else does it show?

"The vase is worth more than I am."

Parents think they have their children's best interests at heart, and they may have. But children have their own interests and priorities, and they have as much right to them as to their own feelings. This doesn't mean that children can do whatever they want. But when you find yourself in conflict with your child, ask yourself whether what the child wants to do jeopardizes his or her health and safety or violates your legitimate rights. If your answer to both questions is no, I suggest you let the child do it.

If you refuse to let your child do something simply because you prefer that he or she not do it, you may need to do some work on your feelings. What happened to you in the past that control, propriety, thrift, or neatness means so much? Who modeled such rigid behavior for you? Who gave you such high hurdles to jump?

Fourth, don't punish—discipline. Which means, set boundaries.

The difference between punishment and discipline is that punishment happens after the fact, for reasons that weren't made clear ahead of time. It is arbitrary and sometimes grossly excessive, and it belittles the child by depriving him or her of the means of controlling the world. Discipline, on the other hand, happens ahead of time, is explicit, and encourages growth by establishing meaningful choices.

Punishment says to a twelve-year-old, "Your room's a perfect mess. What am I going to do with you? You never do what I want. No camp for you this summer! That's all you understand."

Discipline tells a teenager, "If the car isn't cleaned up by two o'clock, you won't be able to use it this weekend." Discipline establishes line-in-the-sand boundaries and gives the child the choice of respecting them or taking the consequences. If the child elects to take the consequences, that is his or her right. The parent should exact the consequences matter-of-factly, without browbeating or shaming the child.

Fifth, never whip, hit, paddle, spank, beat, slap, cuff, pinch, or otherwise physically abuse your child. Never.

Never send a child to bed without dinner, including dessert. Never punish your child through his or her body.

WHEN YOUR CHILD IS ANGRY

Encourage him, encourage her, to express the feeling.

As I've said, young children do this naturally until they're punished for it. Children respond in the moment. When they are angry, they throw themselves on the floor and kick their heels; they shout, they cry, they rage. They don't "judge" their feeling—they feel it. They don't escape into their intellects and say, "Now, just a minute here. Obviously something is troubling me deeply, and if I think it through, I'm sure I can understand it so well I won't feel it anymore."

They get their feelings out through their body. Ten minutes later, they are whistling or playing a game or fretting about something else—anyhow, they are into a whole different set of feelings. They responded to their anger at the moment it occurred by relieving the stressful energy in their bodies, then quickly moved on.

You want to encourage your child's natural response. Certainly don't deny what he feels—by saying, for example, "You're not angry." You don't want to judge her feeling—by saying dubiously, "What are you angry about?" (Which means, "Give me a good enough reason, and maybe I'll let you be angry.") You don't want to shame or punish the child for feeling and for expressing the feeling—by saying, "You stop it! That's no way to behave. I'm ashamed of you. You used to be such a good child. If you don't stop, I'm going to send you to your room. Or thrash your bottom, so you'll really have something to wail about."

If the angry child is too young to understand what you're saying, embrace him, hold him, hug him, comfort him, talk gently to him. If the infant is having a tantrum and struggles to get free, put her down—gently, calmly—so that she can move, making sure that she can't hurt herself. And then stay with the child, leaning over him, so he can see you. Show that you love the child no matter how furious she is. Show that you can be with him in his anger, without judging or punishing him. Say things like, "Yes, yes, little one, you cry. You cry all you need to. I'm here. I'm not going away. I want to be with you, however angry you are."

When your child understands speech, say the same kind of things.

And guide your child toward appropriate ways to express his or her anger, saying things like:

"I can see you're angry. I want you to know I love you. I support you and your anger. Be just as angry as you feel."

"Can you make an ugly, angry face? A face that shows how angry you are? Try it! Oh, that's good. That's so angry!"

"Take these crayons—the light ones or the dark ones or any ones you want—and draw me a picture of how angry you are."

"Take this red plastic bat and hit that couch as hard as you can. That's good! Hit it again and again, just as hard as you can." (Always praise the child's emotional release. Say, "That's fine! You're really hitting it hard. Hit it even harder if you want to." Don't say, "You're not hitting very hard. Can't you do better?")

"Cry! Just go on and cry. That's the best thing to do. Get all your anger out. Right here and now. Keep crying till you feel better. I won't do anything. I'm going to stay with you, if you let me, so you know I support you and want to be close to you. "

If the child is having a tantrum and tells you to go away, do so, saying something like, "Anger is tough, but I know you're going to handle it fine." Never punish—or praise—your child for having a tantrum.

"Twist this towel as hard as you can, and put all your anger into it."

"Scream into this pillow. No one will hear you —not that anyone is listening. Even I will hardly hear you. But I'll be here with you, because I want to be close to you,"

"Do whatever you need to get rid of your anger—provided it doesn't hurt you or anybody else. The most important thing you can do when you're feeling angry or sad is to feel it and express it with your body so you get rid of it. But whatever you do or don't do, I'm going to love you, just as I always do, even if I don't always show you in the right way."

Imagine how different our lives would be if our parents had said things like this to us!

From *Facing the Fire: Experiencing and Expressing Anger Appropriately.* Copyright 2003 by JL Creative Services and John Lee. All rights reserved. JLCS, P.O. Box 769, Woodstock, GA 30188

When I read the book *Radical Honesty,* I knew I had to meet the author, Brad Blanton. I attended several of his workshops and found them quite helpful in allowing me to take off a few of the masks I'd put on over the years. I asked Brad to share some of his story as only he can. I think you'll find that he's—honest.

Turning Stumbling Blocks into Stepping Stones

by Brad Blanton

"Do we see who we are, finally? Do we see, behind the curtain, the scars and insecurities that have controlled us? And when we see them and look them squarely in the eye, do they lose their power over us, backing down from their bullying bluster? Indeed they do. We become free to take our life in whatever shape it has become, and find a good and enjoyable use for it, serving others and ourselves."

—Granny D (Doris Haddock)

I was nine years old when my youngest brother was born. My mother had four miscarriages caused by my stepfather's beating her. My baby brother Mike was born prematurely, also after a beating, and survived. I was his primary caretaker from his birth in 1949 until early in his fifth year in 1953. Our family, headed by drunks who were themselves children, broke up when I was thirteen, as a result of many events, including my twelve-year-old brother and I fracturing my stepfather's skull and breaking three of his ribs before leaving home. After that therapeutic event and a few more like it with my stepfather—and sixteen years of psychotherapy—I'm almost over having my reactions to how I was parented completely run my life.

As Tom Robbins, the famous novelist says, it's never too late to have a happy childhood. When I was a child, I developed skills for dealing with my life circumstances which required me to take care of my younger brothers because my mother and stepfather were usually too drunk to do so. My stepfather was

141

violent, and there were a lot of dangerous people who hung out at our house. I learned to be wary, alert, and quick to respond to cues to predict mood and likely behavior changes in alcoholics, so I could keep them from killing each other or hurting one of the kids. I considered myself a smart kid and a hero and I couldn't afford to admit to being scared and sorry for myself. As a psychologically reactive, homemade, individual humanoid, I ended up wanting to help people, defend them, take care of them, teach them how to take care of themselves, and show off my perceptiveness.

Most of this was a matter of pure luck. I had the dumb luck of my father dying when I was six years old. Then, also by chance, my mother remarried when I was seven to an alcoholic wife beater and child abuser. Because of the same luck, my youngest brother was born when I was nine. Because of all this dumb luck, I became sensitized to subtle cues about human behavior, and also wanted to try to help people who were hurting. I am designed by my life to be a helper who wants to keep those already hurt from being hurt more, and as I grew older I learned to purchase allegiance by helping others. I charge this allegiance to the helpee in an inexplicit way, such that a vague sense of obligation bound them to me, protected me from them, and got me praise. I learned to use it to con people to do what I wanted and to seduce women. I am a manipulative, codependent, lying survivor.

I have here a hand-built, home-built set of neurotic survival techniques, my carried-around-with-me-at-all-times way of getting along feeling protected and surviving set of tools. By transforming my relationship to this fine system of survival instead of being victimized by it, criticizing it, and resisting it, or trying to "fix" it, I can decide to serve people of my own free will, much like the mythical hero Sisyphus, of Greek mythology.

Sisyphus, who used to be a hell of a man and a hero like Hercules and Pan all rolled up into one, when he was on Earth, violated one of the most sacred taboos of the gods by making love to a goddess. He was snatched up and thrown into a special hell forever (just as we, who were once happy as children, have been thrown into the hell of the meaningless meaning-making machine of the mind and the obligations of adult life). Albert Camus wrote that Sisyphus' condition of being condemned for eternity to roll a big boulder up a mountain and have it roll back down again was a perfect analogy for the human condition. We are all condemned to engage in completely futile tasks that take everything we've got, until the day we die. If we are to discover the secret to happiness as human beings, said Camus, we must be able to imagine some way Sisyphus could come to be a happy man, while living in that special hell. Let's say we catch a glimpse of him just as he turns to walk back down that mountain to find the rock and push it up again, and we see a beaming smile on his face. How could that be?

Camus said there could only be one way such a thing could be accomplished. Sisyphus was condemned to the hell of rolling that rock up and having it fall back down, for all eternity, as his punishment, but he conquered hell by transforming his relationship to what he was condemned to do by choosing to do it. Sisyphus decided to choose to do what he was condemned to do. He said, "This is my job, this is what I do for a living, I am good at it; it is what I do. I roll my rock up my mountain and back down again. This is what I do and I'm doin' it."

I, Brad Blanton, can choose to serve people as a design for my life simply because it is a good choice given my design, which I am condemned to live with. I can escape the oppression of the historical personality that drives me even though I cannot escape the personality itself. That is, the meaning made for me without any choice on my part from the life, times, family, and culture I was born into and formed by, was not under my control. What is under my control is the use of that personality. By using the equipment I now luckily have available to me, I can choose to serve people.

To summarize: I learned to survive by taking care of some people and being wary, paranoid, and defending against other people. I will always operate from that mode, and I have no choice in the matter. Still, serving people can be a choice for me and can be very fulfilling and fun if I go about it in a certain way. The way I was built to go about serving people was as an oppressed but surviving secret hero, acknowledged by few, a staunch defender of the helpless who also is a con man—kind of a combination of the Lone Ranger and Jesus and a used-car salesman. I can have that paradigm use me and I will still be a victim of my psychological conditioning. Or, I can choose to use that model to create a life with. However, if I consider myself to be this being-in-the-moment who is typing now, and my history to be something my present-tense self possesses, I can use my memory, in the present, to design a future to live from. I do that by choosing to do what I have been condemned to do. Rather than continue to function from and react to the past that designed how I should live at about age seven or eight or nine, I can transform my life by my own design, by choosing to do what I have been condemned to do. I get to use my personality to bring about my dreams for the future. Instead of trying to fix myself, or change myself, I can simply use myself to create the life I want and to contribute to others the way I want.

And one of the main ways I want to serve people is to present to them the possibility that we are all alike in the way I have just described. To teach that what is true for everybody is that we can have either an unconscious reactive life or a conscious creative life.

This choice to do what one is condemned to do is called transformation. My life is transformed by my choice to serve people because the purpose of my service is no longer to manipulate and control them to get what I want.

I changed my identity from the case-history personality I just described, and now identify myself as the being who notices and who lives in each moment. As a being, who notices, who lives in the moment and is satisfied in the present, I already have everything I want. By giving up the demand that other people make up for how I was deprived, I don't actually need to be compensated anymore, so I just drop the relentless demand and be happy with what I've got.

So, being of unsound mind, as is herein amply demonstrated, and using that to create a future, *I DO DECLARE: MY LIFE IS TO SERVE PEOPLE, BECAUSE I SAY SO.*

The way I serve people is by writing books and conducting seminars to teach people about transcending their story of who they are and becoming creators of their own lives by choosing to do what they are condemned to do. This all comes about through something called Radical Honesty. Radical Honesty is about telling the truth about what you have done, what you think and what you feel, moment to moment. It leads to freedom from the jail of your own mind and the jail of your own history.

My main seminar is an eight-day-long residential workshop called *The Course in Honesty.* There are small communities of people who participate in radical honesty practice groups all over the U.S. and some places in Europe.

Books by Brad Blanton

Radical Honesty: How to Transform Your Life by Telling the Truth

Practicing Radical Honesty: How to Complete the Past, Live in the Present and Build a Future with a Little Help from Your Friends

Honest to God (with Neale Donald Walsch)

Radical Parenting: Seven Steps to a Functional Family in a Dysfunctional World

The Truthtellers: Stories of Success by Radically Honest People

Yoga Saved My Life

Yoga saved my life by *showing* me my life. I was living in a vacuum, a hollow man running on empty. Where was the time to breathe? To think? To feel? I had no clue. I was like Mr. Duffy in the James Joyce novel *Ulysses*. As Joyce so aptly put it: Mr. Duffy lived only a short distance from his body. I began to change only when counselor Vicki Gannon had the nerve to look at me and say, "Guy, you need to get a life."

That comment led to an anger management workshop with John Lee. He gave me permission to be angry, and then taught me how to express my anger appropriately. It was the beginning of the great release.

That led to another workshop with Brad Blanton who gave me permission to be honest—radically honest. I sat in a teepee in Albuquerque, New Mexico and shared my deepest secrets with fifteen other people. And while that experience was healing, something else happened which would change my life.

The workshop participants gathered each morning for yoga. From the first stretch, I knew this was for me. It's been said the first step toward a spiritual life is to get in touch with your body. There's a phrase you'll hear a lot in yoga: *Listen to your body.* My body had been talking to me for many years. It had tried to get my attention with anxiety attacks, backaches, and long episodes of depression, but I refused to take time to listen. It was only when the pain became too intense to ignore that I knew I must listen and change—or else.

It has been my experience that some of the people with the worst problems eventually become strongest in the areas where they were the weakest. Little wonder that I became a yoga instructor. I immersed myself in body, mind and spirit.

After spending most of my life looking for answers out there somewhere, I finally began to look inside. If you come to my yoga classes, you'll occasionally hear me say, "Less is more."

The lessons I've learned from the mat are countless. And perhaps the greatest lesson I've learned is how I hurt myself by wanting more. I wanted to look a certain way in a pose, so I forced my body to do what it could not do at that time. The result—injury. Is it not the same in life? We're constantly asking our bodies to do more than is humanly possible, and we wonder why we get sick or injure ourselves.

The mat has taught—and still is teaching me—honesty and sensitivity. To honor my body for what it can do—and what it cannot do. If we were to sit for an hour and do nothing but breathe, that would be enough. If we were to sit for an hour and listen to our hearts beat, that would be enough. How long has it been since you listened to your heart?

Note: If you would like to learn more about my yoga classes and retreats, visit my web site at www.guyatchley.com

The Yogi

Carlos Castañeda once wrote that in deciding which path to take in life there is only one question you need ask: Does the path have a heart? Darren Rhodes has found his path. At the age of thirty-one, Darren owns two yoga studios in Tucson, Yoga Oasis and Yoga Oasis East. Many people come to yoga to help them deal with physical issues. Darren relates beautifully with these people, and when we sat down for an interview, I soon found out why.

DR: Throughout my childhood my mom practiced and taught yoga in our house. I'd often walk through the living room while she was teaching a class. It was clear to me then that yoga was both a physical and spiritual practice.

Today I believe that yoga is only a spiritual practice. The physical poses are in themselves beautiful expressions of the heart. By the time I was a senior in high school I had developed a 40 degree C curve in my spine. Wrestling and weight lifting were contributing to the problem. At a yoga workshop my mom had heard that a yogin had found relief from her scoliosis back pain by practicing yoga regularly. This news inspired me to begin practicing five days a week in hopes of decreasing both my back pain and C curve. I had a burning desire to get out of pain and transform my back.

The practice I embraced was very demanding. Instead of decreasing my back pain it sometimes made it feel worse. It wasn't until I found my teacher John Friend, the founder of Anusara Yoga, that things began to shift significantly. Being John's student has been one of the greatest blessings of my life.

I am so fortunate to know and be guided by such a great being. John gave me alignment techniques that little by little brought balance and relief to my back pain. More importantly he helped me to change attitude about my scoliosis. He taught me to regard it as a blessing, a gift from God. Now that the curve in my spine is less than ten degrees I do indeed feel that the whole process of transformation was such a gift. It has been an amazing character builder. What I deemed an obstacle became the source of intense growth and inspiration.

About the same time I met John I also found Marie Hanson, a true healer. She's a one-of-a-kind. When I first walked into her space she made it clear that what she was doing was demolition of the body. She'd dig a crystal into my back and break down the sheet of the bone. She essentially attacked my back. The only way I could bear it was to scream and scream. I'd leave with welts and deep bruises. And yet I knew it was this type of intensity along with my intense yoga practice that was going to transform my spine. It took about fifty agonizing sessions with Marie over the span of two years to drastically decrease my C curve. I have an old x-ray which confirms my spine has shifted several inches over. Marie says it's shifted about 4–5 inches. It was extreme enough that others with such a curve have gotten operations. Both John and Marie told me to expect a miracle, and that's what I got. One primary benefit of this transformation is that I can now meditate without pain. Meditation has become a key part of my *sadhana*. The whole process has been an amazing physical and spiritual journey. It's clear to me that I could not have had the physical shift that I did without opening my heart and trusting grace to support and transform me.

GA: And how has it transformed you spiritually?

DR: As Rumi says, "The cure for pain is in the pain." Whenever I'm faced with an obstacle I ultimately see it as a gift. I remember that the obstacle is not eternal. That it's guiding me towards joy. I used to be in pain on a daily basis. It makes the lack of pain such a gift. I don't take my health for granted. There is so much gratitude in my life today.

GA: Has it affected the way you teach yoga?

DR: It helps me relate to and honor students who are dealing with physical, emotional, or spiritual issues in their lives and practices. My story of transformation gives them hope.

GA: What is your goal with the students in your class?

DR: I give them full permission to let go of their limited identity, and to embrace the ocean of goodness within their bodies, minds, and hearts. My classes are challenging. I demand a lot from my students because I know that they are capable of so much.

GA: Why do people come to yoga?

DR: Ultimately I think people come seeking a deeper connection to their own hearts, their own truth. Even those that come just to get a good workout usually stick around because of the emotional and spiritual benefits. A yoga studio can serve as a true community, a place where people connect on a heart level. Life-long friendships and marriages are made at yoga studios.

GA: We have a picture of you standing on your hands and your feet touching your head. Can you tell us something about this pose.

DR: It's called the scorpion. It's a very advanced pose, not something you'll find in most classes. It's an extreme expression of aligning with all parts of ourselves and creation; both the light and the dark. On the scale of evolution humans and scorpions are about as distant as you can get. This pose celebrates all parts of creation as forms of pure consciousness.

GA: Your advice for people thinking of doing yoga?

DR: Do it. Start today. Try out different teachers and styles. You will know it right away when you find the teacher and style you are looking for.

GA: What do you think keeps some people from trying yoga?

DR: Some people feel like it somehow conflicts with their religious beliefs because it has ties with eastern philosophy and religion. It's important for people to know that most styles of yoga ask people to affirm and strengthen rather then change their beliefs. What's so great about yoga is that is creates a non-dogmatic but very spiritual environment. Instead of different beliefs separating each other, it becomes a source of acceptance and connection. Some people also feel self-conscious about their bodies. All the better reason to practice. You'll adore your body in no time.

GA: *Why don't we close with one of your favorite quotes.*

DR: "What is the body? That shadow of a shadow of your love that somehow contains the whole universe." Rumi

Author's note: My thanks to Darren for allowing me to teach at Yoga Oasis East. He's one of my primary teachers, and certainly an inspiration.

It Is Always and Only God

In the summer of 2003, I journeyed to Ibiza, Spain for a yoga retreat with Godfrey Devereux. I had read his books on yoga and found them incisive and inspiring. For three weeks I lived in a tent with no phone, no fax, no computer. It was a break I desperately needed. After five hours of yoga each morning, I spent afternoons on Benirras Beach and ended each day with a picture postcard sunset.

It's important to state here that yoga is not a religion, but it can greatly enhance your religious life, or spiritual quest, or your life in general simply by helping you see what's really happening. I came away from Can Am having reconciled some long-standing issues about the Infinite. It was quite surprising to me, considering Godfrey was not the yogi I'd envisioned. He was human, humorous, and occasionally profane, but above all, he was honest.

GA: *What is your education?*

GD: I had the best education English money could buy.

GA: *And that is?*

GD: Well, I went to one of the five exclusive English public schools, the one that according to my father has as its fundamental educational ethos to help you to learn, to think for yourself—Marlborough. It's what we call public schools, which means it's private.

GA: *So, when did you get out of Marlborough?*

GD: When I was sixteen.

GA: *From there where did you go?*

GD: From there I went into a solo exploration of the nature of consciousness.

GA: *Which means?*

GD: I got into doing yoga and LSD.

GA: *Oh, really? And how long did that last?*

GD: Well, the yoga is still going thirty years later. The LSD lasted intensely about five years and stopped completely after eight years.

GA: *And was that the limit of your drug experience, or were there other drugs?*

GD: Well, I smoked marijuana during that period, but my main interest was with what happened when I took LSD.

GA: *Just finding out what was there?*

GD: Well, the thing was, the first time I did LSD on my own, I did yoga for eight hours. So, the two became fairly deeply inter-linked. I'd done LSD maybe three times before at festivals and I did this trip and I did yoga the whole time and at the end of it—I didn't know that I did—but I knew everything about Indian wisdom, and I knew it and I started talking about it to my friends about reincarnation and we are all one and all this stuff and I never read any of this stuff. But because I was doing yoga while I was tripping that's where the acid took me...with that understanding.

GA: *So you learned something from your trips?*

GD: Yeah, I learned that we create our own reality or you could put it now that reality is a projection existing in the mind. And the senses reveal only a tiny part of the amount of data that's available to consciousness. All kinds of things. And I didn't necessarily quantify or understand it the way I do now. But I would say that what yoga has done is allowed me to embody the wisdom that drugs gave me, if you see what I mean. To embody it, so it wasn't just conceptual, you know I can see through taking

153

drugs certain things. But the implications of that, in terms of how you live your life, drugs don't give you. But yoga has over the thirty years brought me to a similar state of consciousness today without the weirdness. I'm no longer just relating to the surface appearance, even though that's all I'm seeing.

GA: *Were you ever addicted to a drug?*

GD: I never took a physically addictive drug, so I only took drugs that are not physically addictive. I made an agreement with myself when I was very young before I started that I wouldn't take addictive drugs. I didn't trust myself to stay alive if I did that.

GA: *And why did you STOP taking drugs?*

GD: I stopped smoking cannabis basically because it became boring. And I didn't enjoy the effect anymore, the novelty wore off. The last time I took LSD I sat in lotus posture for eight hours in a sanctuary in a holy house, in a holy place. And I could feel very, very clearly within my body that the energy that was fueling the movements of my consciousness was coming out of the cells in my body. And I could feel it weakening. So then I didn't have to think. There was no question that I would never do it again.

GA: *What years are we talking about?*

GD: That was 1980 or '81.

GA: *Were you a hippy?*

GD: I was a hard-core hippy (laughs).

GA: *And how have you evolved from that?*

GD: I am a hard-core hippy (more laughter). In terms of values, yes, definitely. But I was being somewhat ironic by saying I am a hippy. If you think love and peace means you can push me around, think again.

GA: *How did you discover yoga, or how did yoga discover you?*

GD: I left school when I was sixteen because of my involvement with drug-taking and this was just before we're supposed to take our A-level, which were the examinations in those days that you had to pass in order to go to universities. So, in order to still do those, my parents sent me to stay with my uncle to carry on preparing myself for the examinations on my own. And I used to do it in this sanctuary. He was a minister of the Church of England, and one day in the afternoon, he was standing there in tree pose in a pair of boxer shorts with his palms together in front of his chest in front of the altar. Now, my uncle was the only adult, really, that I ever met whom I could relate to. He had a fantastic sense of fun and this amazing ability to communicate to anybody. And I got on with him very well, and he was probably the only adult, at that time, that I'd be open and honest with what I really thought. And I walked in and I could feel something coming off him and I wanted it. I felt this very peaceful vibration, and within it was only what I could say is reverence. As a minister it was obviously directed towards Jesus or God.

GA: *Is your uncle still alive?*

GD: Still alive, still stands on his head sometimes. I dedicated my first book to him and three other people, so he has a copy. He told me he used to go around to every library demanding that they get a copy to boost my sales.

GA: *I heard why you were drawn to yoga. Why are the people who go to your retreats drawn to yoga?*

GD: I don't know. And I don't think that you could point to a common factor, but I think they're all drawn to Can Am by forces unknown to them. It's very few people who come to Can Am, who find it unpalatable, but there are many in the yoga world who find me unpalatable and would find what we do there unpalatable.

GA: *Because?*

GD: Because I'm outspoken, because I tell the truth, because I do not subscribe to the orthodoxy of the church. So those who have a deep investment, whether in their own practice or whatever, they get that feeling about me and they don't want to have their path upset.

GA: So, for some people yoga is like a religion to them?

GD: Well, not overtly, but they bring to it or they use it to develop their own belief system. Whereas yoga is fundamentally a way to see into the pragmatic nature of a belief system. That's about all it is, it has a pragmatic value or not. It doesn't have an absolute value. But people put absolute values on their beliefs. They say you shouldn't eat meat. I eat meat. You shouldn't wear leather. I wear leather. You shouldn't curse, well…

GA: During a retreat, you said you had seriously considered not being a yoga teacher anymore.

GD: Well, I… yeah, I tried to get out of it (laughs), fundamentally because I didn't like being put up on a pedestal. When people put me up on a pedestal, as if I could answer every question under the sun, you know, and as if I had solved all the mysteries of life, I didn't like it because I felt that they were disempowering themselves. It didn't bother me what they thought of me particularly; it bothered me that, even in my unwilling participation in that dynamic, they were disempowering themselves, then what I thought could benefit them was not really happening. So that was the problem. And I didn't see a way around it. And so, a few years ago, I had a three-day crisis. I spent it on the beach, and I had this dialogue with myself: Do you want to do this? Why do you want to do that? One option is to live a nice quiet island life for ten years and forget about being a yoga teacher, or I could take my money and invest it in the center. But anyway, I realized I had to carry on. The same people were still putting me up on a pedestal and I wasn't liking it, but I came to some kind of superficial realization that I had to carry on.

GA: You say that yoga is the most dangerous form of exercise, because you get into a position that you don't normally get into, and you stay there. I read an article from a doctor who said he had not seen so many injuries from a fitness craze since the Jane Fonda aerobics days of the '80s.

GD: Totally.

GA: So, give me your thoughts on that and how it could be prevented.

GD: Well, if yoga was approached in the way yoga is designed to be approached, then it wouldn't be a problem. But it's approached as a physical exercise; therefore, people are concerned with the physical results. Hence, they're trying to get more movement or they're trying to get more strength. But it's the movement thing that causes most of the injuries. They're trying to get more flexibility, and they don't have any understanding of the body so they're making their ligaments and joints do stuff that they can't. And if they could realize that yoga is not really a physical medium, it just has a physical aspect, and that physical aspect should be approached according to the rules. Rule number one is sensitivity; number two is honesty. You must have sensitivity and honesty about what you're capable of, then those injuries wouldn't happen. Those injuries don't happen to my students—at least not in my presence.

GA: What do you hope your students take away from Can Am?

GD: Well, I hope they don't take away anything that was here (laughs). What would I like them to take away? I'd like them to take away well-being. I'm offering people space really. A psychological space for them to hopefully learn to appreciate who they are and the life that's happening. That's what I see of the potential value of what I do really. More specifically I could say I'd like them to take away the understanding that—it is always and only God.

GA: "It is always and only God." What does that mean?

GD: The "always" means nothing. You can attribute anything to that word you like—feelings, actions, events, situation, an object. There is nothing that is NOT God. So that is what always means. And "only" means the same. There is only God. There is nothing apart from God. God includes everything. "It" means that every little thing in its true self is the whole of God. "Always and only God" means no blame, no guilt, no shame, no pride, no resentment, no regret, no anxiety, no manipulation. So that's the point—peace.

GA: *Have you been able to achieve that?*

GD: It's not something that you can achieve. The natural unfolding of events seems to be such that I have become a stranger to all those tendencies, but I make no assumption that they're not going to pop up any minute now.

GA: *What is the toughest ordeal you had to go through, and how did you deal with it?*

GD: Being separated from my children—especially him. (Godfrey points to his son, Arum, who is tape recording our conversation). How did I deal with it? I don't know. Lived it out. I came to peace with that particularly on his birthday during a Zen retreat. I was meditating and freaking out about the whole thing. I wasn't just freaking out about my relationship with my son, but also freaking out about my relationship with my father, seeing how even though the externality was different, it was the same dynamic. I had been unfathered, even though he hadn't been absent. And so I felt that I didn't know what it meant to father. I came to peace with it because a Buddhist sensei said to me: "Can you tell me this now, Godfrey, that no matter how else you judge anything that you did or didn't do, was there any moment that you didn't do your best?"

And I said, "No."
"Then every moment you did your best?"
And I said, "Yes."
She said, "Then why do you feel bad about it?"
And I said, "Well, I don't—*now.*"

GA: *You're now forty-six. What are you planning for the coming years of your life? Do you have another dream?*

GD: I have no more dreams.

GA: *No more dreams?*

GD: No more dreams. I'll take the dreams that come. But I'm not looking for anything.

Author's note: I love this quote from Godfrey's book, Hatha Yoga: Breath by Breath:

> Every moment of your life
> every event that you participate in or witness
> every word you hear or read
> can enrich you
> if you meet if fully, openly
> and with love

Godfrey Devereux's new yoga home is in the Tuscan Mountains National Park near Bibbiena, Italy. For more information go to www.windfireyoga.com.

Near-Death Experiencers

In 1998 I sat in a studio with some extraordinary people. All of them have gone through near-death or out-of-body experiences—the result of tragic occurrences. These people were on the brink of death when they saw a tunnel and a bright light and communicated with a presence, which they give various names: the being, the entity, the higher power—God. These Near Death Experiencers, or NDE'ers, are quite accustomed to people not believing them. Skeptics say this experience is nothing more than the brain short-circuiting because of the trauma. And it may be. But these people come back with some amazing stories.

It happened more than two decades ago. Fritzi Carp-Ruiz was riding on the back of a motorcycle. Her then husband was driving fifty miles per hour when the cycle blew a tire and began skidding on its side. Fritzi was wearing a helmet that cracked in two with the impact of her head on the pavement.

That's when something happened. It was as though Fritzi could feel herself slipping out of her body and looking down on the accident scene. She began watching the cycle as it continued to slide. She saw the young woman lying there and thought to herself—that must hurt. Then Fritzi realized *she* was the young woman. A golden light surrounded her with warmth and peace. And then she heard a voice say, "You have to go back."

Fritzi woke up in excruciating pain. Later, she went through a period of depression, but the near-death experience stayed with her. On an Easter Sunday she went to a church where she had another strange experience. During the altar call, it was as if a dome opened above her, and there once again she saw the

160

light. Two hundred people were there, but only Fritzi was having this experience. In the midst of the light was a three-dimensional shadow, and that shadow was telling Fritzi to "continue the journey, and know that you are loved." Fritzi's journey led her to work with hospice patients. She has a unique perspective on what they're going through. She feels as though she's been there.

This story is made even more remarkable by something else that Fritzi remembers from the accident. Her husband's motorcycle was a custom bike with an Indian-head nickel glued on the side. Fritzi informed her husband that she could tell him exactly where the nickel had come to rest after the impact jarred it from the bike. In her altered state she had seen it roll away. When they went back to the scene of the crash, Fritzi did not hesitate. She walked directly to an eerily familiar rock and looked under it. There on the ground was a gleaming Indian-head nickel.

Terry Oberto's truck rolled three times throwing him out the back window and into the light.

Terry told me, "If you took a thousand people and asked them to describe the most joyous, blissful, euphoric moments in their lives, then you added up all those experiences and multiplied them a hundred times, it would still not even come close to the way this felt for me."

Having said that, Oberto adds, "What's important is not the event, but what happens *after* the event."

Many of the people who go through this kind of experience are changed forever. They are no longer afraid of death. They're not hung up on material things. And they find beauty everywhere they look. They're able to see the miraculous in the simple, and they're no longer bothered by life's little stressors. They've resigned as general managers of the world, and they're content to let the universe take care of itself.

As Terry says, "If I can get up and walk and breathe, everything else is a plus."

When I interviewed Mary Brave Bird, the author of *Lakota Woman* and *Ohitika Woman*, she described her near-death experience. Doctors told her she had been dead for about twenty seconds before they brought her back to life. She had crashed her car into a telephone pole. During open-heart surgery she had a vision. In her vision she visited her grandma who had raised her. She said, "Grandma, I came to stay with you. I don't want to stay in the world anymore. I miss you."

Her Grandma replied, "No, you can't. You have kids to take care of. Think of them. You have to go back. I'll be here for you when you're ready to come over. I'll always be here for you."

Mary did come back, and today she spends much of her time encouraging the young people of her tribe. Her message for every person she meets is simple: only one person can put limitations on your life—and that person is you.

David Ralph saw a bright light during his near-death experience. David, at thirty-nine years old, lives with Duchenne Muscular Dystrophy. Few patients with the illness survive as long as he has. A tracheotomy allows him to breathe, but he has to sway back and forth to help his lungs pull in air. At night he breathes with the help of a respirator. His legs and feet are useless and his hands have only a little strength. In May, 1987 David's heart stopped for a few minutes, but doctors were able to bring him back to life. During his brush with death David saw a bright light and heard the voice of his mother who had died of cancer four years before. She told him to go back.

David told me, "I feel as though I came back for a purpose. I just don't know what the purpose is."

At that point I looked around the room. David had an entire wall covered with letters and cards from people who have come to know him and to love him—people whose lives he has touched.

I said, "Let me suggest that the reason you're here is to inspire others. What greater calling could anyone have?"

"Maybe so," he said, "Maybe that's why we're all here."

All these near-death experiencers seem to come back with this overriding message: *Only one thing matters—and that is love.*

The Wall

*On Veterans Day 1994, I was in Washington, D.C.
with seventeen Vietnam veterans from Tucson. All
of them suffered from Post-Traumatic Stress Disorder.
Some had experienced flashbacks and nightmares
for more than two decades. This was their journey
of healing.*

What is the source of our first suffering? It lies in the hesitation to speak. It was born in the moments when we accumulated silent things within us. —Colette Gaudin

Rick Church—In His Words

My experience in Vietnam was like a dream. It was just like a black and white dream. It's so hard to relate to some of the things I did. I found myself in a position doing things that I would see on TV when I was a kid, like digging graves and burying bodies. Sometimes the bodies didn't fit in the graves, so I'd take an E tool and break their legs so they would fit. I mean, this was so unreal that it was just like a state of shock for months and months and months.

I went into a tunnel one time as a tunnel rat and ended up feeling someone's face, and I shot into the face. I was covered with skull, and scalp, and blood and hair. I remember flies dancing on my face, eating that stuff, and I couldn't hear from the concussion of the round going off, and in some of my dreams I'll wake up, and I'll go into the bathroom and wash my face, and I never understand why.

When I eventually got out of Vietnam we weren't treated very well. We wanted to talk about our experiences, but we were told by friends and adults not to talk about it. The message was: It's over with, you don't have to bring it up; you don't ever have to live it again. My problem was I went about twenty to twenty-five years without talking about it, and nightmares and stuff started happening, and I really needed some help. So I contacted people at the Vet Center in Tucson, and I told them I'm having flashbacks, I'm having terrible dreams, I want to know if this is normal. What they told me is yeah, that is normal for somebody who's been in Vietnam and hasn't talked about it for dozens of years, and all of a sudden they're reliving things, they're seeing things. I can honestly say there hasn't been one day go by in twenty-five years that I haven't thought about Vietnam at least once. You smell something, or you hear something, or you eat something, and right away you remember Vietnam.

I remember when I first got back from Vietnam. It was winter in Wisconsin, and I had outgrown all of my clothes. When I went into the Marine Corps, I was young, and narrow, and skinny, but when I got out, I was pretty well beefed up. I had all this combat pay to spend, so I bought a nice wardrobe. I had a cashmere overcoat on, and I'm walking past this restaurant with these huge plate glass windows, and a school bus comes by and backfires, and I hit the deck right away. It was muddy, slushy, you know, city slime in the winter. I got up, and looked in the restaurant, and people in the restaurant were laughing, and I thought you assholes. This was the start of it. I couldn't explain why I did what I did. It was a response, that's all it was.

I reached a point where I wouldn't talk about Vietnam. People would ask me if I was in the service, and I'd deny it. They would ask me things about Vietnam, or what I thought about Vietnam, and I would offer no opinions.

A lot of the guys I know turned to drugs, a lot of guys turned to alcohol, I know a lot of guys who died in Vietnam. They sent the shell home, and they told the shell don't talk about it, just be quiet about it. If you don't bring it up, nobody else will talk about it. It's something you really shouldn't talk about.

I've been putting off going to the wall for years and years. The closest I've ever gotten, Davis Monthan Air Force Base had a mock-up of the wall at one of their air shows. I went in there with a list of guys I wanted to see on the wall. I got to the first one, and I couldn't do it anymore. My daughter was with me. She was little, and I heard her say to her friend, my dad's crying. I thought that's it. Never again will I cry in front of my kid. So I took her hand, and I walked out of that hangar. I couldn't stand being in there. I was going to be stoic, I was going to be the father, I was never going to shed a tear over this crap, especially when my kids could see me. Another mistake. I realize what I really got to do. I got to go to the wall. I think I have to see the wall to make sure I'm not on that thing.

David Blevins—In His Words

I went to Vietnam in April 1969. I went to Vietnam as a nineteen-year-old, right out of high school really; just a normal kid was what I was, and now I got to survive by killing people. I had a lot of ideals and standards in Vietnam that were all shot to hell, literally; they don't apply, everything was backwards. After my very first fire fight in Vietnam, I puked my guts out. After about the third fire fight, I got a little sick to my stomach, by about the fifth, they were just silhouettes; didn't mean anything. It was him or me.

I had a situation where I just came from a mine sweep. It was about three o'clock in the morning, and we had been out for about eight hours now for the last four days in a row, and I was supposed to run ammunitions that morning at five o'clock in the morning, and I was just exhausted. One of the guys in my outfit volunteered, and we kind of worked it out. He says I'll pull some duty for you, so him and his shotgun took ammunition to Bienhut. To my knowledge they never made it back. I felt guilty about that, because I felt he died in my place. Since doing a lot of work at the vet center, a lot of stuff has come up, and there's a strong possibility he didn't die. I don't know, I cannot remember the man's name. It's been a total block for the last twenty-five years; I cannot remember the guy's name.

So, going to the wall for me is a mission, hopefully the last one. I just want to say I'm sorry, I failed, and I apologize. Please forgive me. I'm sorry I was tired that night.

In 1970 I came back to the U.S. I was by myself on the plane, no buddies to come home with, no outfit to come home with. I went over there by myself, and I came back by myself. There was absolutely no counseling. You're back in the U.S., thank you, good-bye.

I was in the Tucson Airport when there was a protest against the war. Somebody spit on me, and I was prepared to kill him. He pulled me by the arm and turned me around, and he asked me if I was coming from Vietnam, and I said yeah, and I attempted to walk away. I've had my confrontations, and I don't need anymore, I've had my fill. But still he grabbed my arm again, and he asked me point-blank if I killed any babies over there, and if I remembered what they looked like. I didn't answer the question. I just stared at him, and I was asking myself—why is that guy asking me that question? Then he hollered "baby killer" and spit on me. Instinct. It was like he just pulled a knife or a gun on me. I went for his throat. The security guards came running over, and there was a big altercation. Being a big man like I am, I wasn't going to let go. I had his throat, and I knew where to push to crush his throat, and he was turning white. They finally broke my grip, and I snapped out of it, and thought oh, this is where I am, I can't do that here. So I explained the situation, I just got out of Vietnam two days ago—forty-eight hours. "Let me go home, get this guy out of my face!"

They escorted me out and I met my folks. My mother helped me unpack my bags. I'm now twenty years old. She pulled out some medals I had received, and I told her you don't want to know about them, don't ask, and she's never asked.

People look at Vietnam veterans as some kind of animal, and if you get told often enough you're an animal or a piece of crap, you start believing it.

In 1984 I attempted suicide. I couldn't figure things out anymore; I couldn't handle things anymore. I realized in 1985, with the fall of Saigon, the ten-year anniversary, I needed help; otherwise, I would be dead.

Even to this point in time, my death to me is inconsequential, it means very little. It's a sad thing to say. I don't fear it, I don't look forward to it, but I don't fear it. If I were placed in a situation, even today, that if I had to protect somebody to die, I would do it without any hesitation. You can't hurt me. If I die, I die; it's inevitable. It's something that's got to happen. I've seen it, tasted it, know what it smells like. Death has something in the air that's very distinct. Aromas bring back memories. Sights bring back memories. Memories bring back memories. When you're in Vietnam, everything worked. You could feel a hair follicle working, you'd feel it tingling, your fingernails, everything worked. If it didn't, you didn't survive. And to learn that at nineteen, this is what it takes to survive, okay, I guess I'll have to do that to survive.

What bothered me the most when I came back to the U.S. is gee, how could I become an animal so quick, in just a year's time? Don't you have to be exposed to that for a long time before you say screw everything, I'm going to survive? That's not the kind of person I was when I left. That much guilt for that long, you have to let go sooner or later, or you'll destroy yourself. I will try and work it out. I didn't think I could until one marriage, three children, a lot of booze, a lot of drugs had gone by. I'm screwing up me. That's all I'm hurting is me. I came back a forty-year-old man at twenty. I'm now forty-five, and I'm just starting to catch up.

Mike Purvance—In His Words

I was a medic in Vietnam. I came from Provo, Utah, which is a fairly nondemonstrative secular society. I came home, and they said "Okay, Mike, it's done with. You did a good job; get on with your life."

They didn't want to talk about it. So, there was no decompression from the war. That was when I turned to alcohol.

I don't want to sit here and preach about Post-Traumatic Stress Disorder and have anyone feel sorry for us. I mean, especially me, because I'm fighting every single day to accomplish things now that I haven't been able to do in the past. Those of us unlucky enough to have this disorder have absolutely no sense of finality about the war. We fight it everyday. One of the symptoms is flashbacks, a term that they call intrusive thinking. I'm in Vietnam everyday, the same battle over and over again. I just can't get it right.

In battle, when someone was severely injured, severely injured to the point that death was upon them, they didn't want to go home that way. There were a lot of screams like, let me die, I don't want to go home this way. That's why the casualties so many times are a difficult thing for me because we successfully allowed them to go home. Those that died, sometimes I wonder if they weren't better off.

There's one I can remember especially. There was a great sense of sadness that his childhood was taken from him, and it's something that we as adults sitting here talking about Vietnam forget. We're talking twenty-five or thirty years ago, twenty-five or thirty years ago. I was a kid, and so were these people, just kids, eighteen or nineteen years old. It was life taken away from them then. Their youth was taken away, and their future was destroyed.

There are a lot of people on the wall that I know, people that I held in my arms as they died. I have a general, at times almost overwhelming sense of sadness, and that's part of this condition, this post-traumatic stress, I just can't shake it. I have a strong opinion that if these fellows, these comrades in arms, were alive, and were able to see me now, they would say, it's over, get on with your life, And if I could talk to them, I would like to express to them that we went there to do the job that we were told to do. We went there because we were proud to be Americans, and we continue to be proud to be veterans. We care. We cared then, and we care now.

The Eleventh Bullet

Another one of the veterans on the trip to D.C. was John Shewmaker. When John got to Vietnam, one problem he faced was his shaving mirror. It kept breaking while he was on patrol. He wrote home about this, and a few weeks later, his father sent him a small, stainless steel shaving mirror, just the right size for his shirt pocket.

A few weeks later, in the middle of the night, the Viet Cong invaded John's camp. It was a bloodbath. John was the last one alive in his trench. He could see his only chance of survival was to pull the bodies of the other American soldiers on top of him and play dead.

When the Viet Cong came up to the ditch, they emptied their rifles into it just to make sure everyone was dead. Those bullets went through the bodies and into John Shewmaker. He was hit eleven times. One of those bullets would have taken his life. It was headed straight for his heart, but it was stopped by a little stainless steel shaving mirror.

I followed John and the other men to the Vietnam Veterans Memorial. I watched as they touched the black granite wall, embraced one another, and shed tears that had been held inside far too long. Our visit ended with a banquet where every man had the chance to say what the experience had meant to him.

One veteran expressed the consensus when he said, "I thought I was going crazy. I thought I was the only one this was happening to. Now, I know I'm not alone. I know I can survive."

If you bring forth what is within you
What you bring forth will save you.
If you do not bring forth what is within you,
What you do not bring forth will destroy you.

—*The Apocrypha*, St. Thomas, verse 70.

Brief Encounters

You're going to be the same five years from now as you are today, except for two things: the people you meet and the books you read. —Charles Tremendous Jones

The Day I Met Lovingkindness

The old woman sat down beside me in 18-C, frazzled after a day of flying. She was still trying to find space for her cane, a bulky plastic bag, and her straw hat when she looked over and said, "I've come all the way from Tacoma to see my daughter in Tucson."

I instantly felt affection for my fellow traveler because she reminded me of my mother a thousand miles away in Oklahoma.

"Is there anything I could do for you?" I asked.

"Not really. All I need is a good spaghetti dinner. I haven't eaten since this morning. I'm sure my daughter will have a nice meal for me when I get to Tucson. I plan to live there, you know."

I wondered what prompted the move. I didn't have to ask.

"My husband died of lung cancer a few weeks ago," she said. "Cigarettes. I couldn't get him to stop."

I nodded and thought about people in my life with the same habit. I rarely get involved in conversations on airplanes. It's time I reserve for napping or reading, but on this day I didn't need sleep or a book. I'd just come from a yoga retreat in Abiquiu, New Mexico where I'd studied books, enjoyed yoga, and meditated for eight days below the clay cliffs of Ghost Ranch.

One of the meditations I learned focused on *metta*, a Buddhist term for "lovingkindness." I felt a lot of it for this soul in the seat next to me. And to think—we weren't supposed to be sitting next to each other. Or were we? Just a few minutes before, I'd given up my seat across the aisle so a young couple who had received separate seat assignments could be close to one another.

During my stay at Ghost Ranch I'd listened to some of my fellow yoga instructors engage in spirited conversations about such phenomena as synchronicities, seemingly inconsequential happenings that, when viewed with an open mind, could be recognized as tiny miracles in the unfolding of your life. I remained silent and kept that in mind. In my work as a news reporter I've interviewed any number of people whose lives were transformed by inexplicable events. (Those who have had near-death experiences are a good example.)

The flight from Phoenix to Tucson, the last leg of my journey home, was short. Just enough time for my new friend to talk about her plans to get an air conditioner for the hot Arizona summers, and for me to point out a few landmarks, including a place for her to cool off, Mount Lemmon. By the time our plane was on approach, this woman who had been so nervous now seemed at peace and ready to begin her new adventure.

After the plane landed and passengers prepared to disembark, I realized we had not even shared our names.

"By the way, my name is Guy. What's yours?"

"Oh, my mother gave me a terrible name. She called me Medie."

She pronounced it *Meedy* and spelled it out for me: M-E-D-I-E.

"I never knew where it came from," she continued, "but I knew I wasn't going to keep it. So, I changed it."

I smiled and waited for the rest of the story.

"Meta," she said. "My name is Meta."

Never had I met anyone with this name. She spelled it with only one "t" as opposed to the Buddhist word that uses two, but it was close enough for me to ask, "Do you know what *metta* means?"

"No," she replied.

"Lovingkindness," I said.

The corners of Meta's mouth slowly turned up as her eyeglasses magnified a twinkle. Clutching her cane, the old woman hobbled away to her waiting daughter; however, I believe Meta took with her something she didn't have before. And so did I.

Caught up in the mystery of the moment, I forgot my luggage stored in an overhead bin. The bag flew on to destinations unknown; however, what I lost on that flight was nothing compared to what I gained. I now make it a point to look for *metta* in every person I meet.

Hungry for Love

The old man looked as though a good breeze could blow him over. He had reason to be frail. He had almost died from malnutrition. For several months he had eaten nothing but one cupcake a day. Finally, somebody found out what was going on and called a doctor. The eighty-six year old was taken to the hospital and nursed back to health.

When we sat down for an interview, my first question was, "Why?"

The whole time he had not been eating, there was plenty of food in the house.

"Why had he not eaten?"

"Oh, that's simple," he answered. "I didn't eat, because I didn't have anyone to eat with."

The Minister

One of the most wonderful men I ever met was Paul Tunis, an Assembly of God minister who constantly reached out to people in need. It was one of the saddest moments of my life when I learned that Paul had suffered a fatal heart attack. But later, when the people of Victory Assembly of God in Tucson held a memorial service to celebrate Paul's life, I was in awe at the number of people whose lives he had touched.

Paul made it a habit to leave his calling card everywhere he went, including restaurants. He once left his ministry card with a tip for a young waitress who appeared to be distraught. Later that night, he received a call from Karen. She needed to talk.

Paul and Karen met, and she told her story. How she left her family in California to strike out on her own. How she developed a drinking problem. And how she'd been living with a man who finally told her that he didn't want to see her anymore.

Karen said life no longer seemed worth living. She felt as though nobody in the world cared whether she lived or died. Paul was able to convince her that not only did he care, but he was also certain that her family in California also must be concerned about her.

Paul asked if he could call her mother. Karen said yes. Paul dialed the number. Karen's mother answered. Paul said, "I've got somebody here who wants to talk to you."And he handed Karen the phone. For the next few minutes, a mother and her daughter talked together, cried together and formed a new relationship. Karen returned to California and began to create a new life for herself.

That night when she felt so all alone, Karen was holding a bottle of pills that she planned to use to end her life. However, that plan changed dramatically when she remembered something she had in her pocket. It was a calling card left by a man who felt he could make a difference—and did.

A Painter of Peace

It's six a.m., and Mary Schaefer rises to enjoy her garden. There are birds to feed, flowers to smell, colors to enjoy. She draws her strength and inspiration from the solitude, a statement that contains more truth than you might think. A few steps away through French doors is her studio. An easel and brushes await the artist's hand and the stroke of genius.

She makes it look simple, but the artist will tell you it wasn't always so. Some seventeen years ago, in the middle of her life, Mary picked up a pencil and began to sketch. She taught herself at first, then took a few lessons. The pencil became a brush, and pastels became oils. But eventually it was a dream that changed Mary's life and took her artwork to an entirely new level.

In the dream Mary stood in her garden gazing into a brilliantly blue sky which opened into a perfect circle. Sparkling rain drenched her body and spirit and awakened her creativity.

Mary says, "Life is art. I see that every day of my life. Just walk out your back door. I marvel at shapes. I marvel at colors. And I know there's a Supreme Being. There has to be, because no one could have had a palette and brush to do all that you see. I never get tired of the mountains. I see them brand new every day. It's a wonderment to me. And I feel sorry for people who can't see those things. They seem to look past life."

In this world created from Mary's imagination, flowers frame an old Mexican hacienda that really exists down some dirty desert road she once traveled. But in Mary's world, the building takes on a new environment. Pansies and petunias come alive in brilliant reds, yellows and blues.

If you want to see the colors of love, just look at Mary's work. Sometimes people stand in front of her paintings and cry from the feelings they bring out. Others ask to spend time in her studio just to be surrounded by the beauty in scores of paintings.

Mary says, "If I could do anything for anyone, it would be to give them the peace that I feel. I don't know where it comes from, but it's almost like a fountain that I can't stop. And I don't want it to stop. It's a great blessing."

Wings of Freedom

At a wildlife sanctuary near Green Valley, Arizona I learned a valuable lesson about the symbol of our country, the bald eagle.

Sue Simpson, who runs the sanctuary, pointed out she has no problems helping the very young eagles that have been injured. They remain relatively calm in their cages as they heal and regain their strength. But, she says, an adult eagle, when he is placed in a cage, will literally flap himself to death trying to get out.

Sue says the reason is simple. Once the bird is old and has tasted freedom, anything less is not good enough.

Santa's Gift

No one is so poor as to have nothing to give. Give
what you have. To someone it may be better than
you dare think.

Don White loves to play Santa Claus at Christmas time, and he plays the part quite well with his long white beard and round belly. However, there was a time when Don questioned whether he should impersonate the jolly old elf.

Don was self-conscious about his glass eye. He thought it might scare some of the children who sit on his lap at the local mall. Well, it didn't take long for one little girl to notice. She was mesmerized by Don's eye while none of the other kids seemed to notice.

Don made note of what the girl wanted for Christmas, then went to her father and began to apologize for whatever concern Santa's eye might have caused.

The man stopped Don in mid-sentence, and said, "Sir, you have no need to apologize. You don't know what you've done for my daughter. You see, she has a glass eye, too."

I have a friend in Alaska by the name of Victor Fitzgaireld. He's a biologist, and he loves nature. Once during an early morning walk in the Alaskan wilderness, Victor wrote the following words:

Winter's Token

Upon entering this valley
Narrow cut by stream
I enter less a valley
I enter more a dream

Where great cottonwoods shower
Upon the green gray spruce
Golden leaves that overpower
The green of lesser use

Autumn's golden carpet there
Is laid as winter's token
As the silence holds the morning air
The stillness goes unbroken

I know the sounds; I know the scents
That early winter brings to me
I see the sights; I hear the hints
They bear no misery

I am all that I see
And all I see is part of me
All is burned into my heart
God's own nature, God's own art

Vic Fitzgaireld

The Cover-up

Every summer Vic Fitzgaireld flies from his home in Willow, Alaska to see his grandmother in Locust Grove, Oklahoma. Winnifred Littlefield is an extraordinary quilter.

To help his grandmother, Vic recommended that he take one of her quilts back to Alaska, sell it, and send her the money. Well, Vic had the best of intentions, but in Alaska, he just didn't have time to peddle the wares. In the end it was easier for him just to send his grandmother two hundred dollars and let her think someone else had purchased it.

To Vic's surprise, another quilt soon arrived in the mail. Granny Littlefield obviously was excited about the expanding market for her product. Vic couldn't bring himself to tell his grandmother that he was the one buying her quilts. At last report, Granny had made more than a thousand dollars from her new Alaskan outlet.

By the way, if you ever need a good quilt, I know where you can get one at a reasonable price.

Destiny

There is a destiny that makes us brothers,
No one goes his way alone;
For all that we send into the lives of others,
Comes back into our own.   —Edwin Markham

As I sat at the lunch counter a man walked in and took the stool next to me. He looked as though he didn't have a friend in the world. He asked, "How ya doin'?"

"Fine," I said, "And how are you?"

"Not so good," he said, "I need a kidney transplant, or I'm going to die."

I wasn't prepared for that answer. All I could say was, "I'm sorry."

With a bit of optimism he added, "My brother might be able to help me. He might give me one of his kidneys."

"Good," I said.

"But," he added, "My brother and I haven't spoken for fifteen years, and I'm not sure whether I have the nerve to ask him to give me one of his kidneys."

Then the man leaned over and whispered, "If he were in my shape, I'm not sure whether I would help him."

The Sweat Lodge

"Have you really lived ten thousand or more days? Or have you lived one day ten thousand or more times?" This quotation from Dr. Wayne Dyer changed my life. I set about to do some things I hadn't done before.

Occasionally I enter a sweat lodge with several Native American friends, among them Willie Wise Eagle, Jimmy Little Tree, Jimmy Spotted Bear, and Michelle Medicine Woman.

I listen as they offer up prayers to *Wakan Tanka*, the One who lives forever and ever, and prayers of thanks to Mother Earth for all that She provides.

My first experience was a forty-five minute sweat. The experience was intense for several reasons, not the least of which was the heat. When we crawled out of the small teepee, I could not stand up. I was so weak that I tripped and fell. The best I could do was to pull myself onto hands and knees into the grass.

Willie Wise Eagle studied me for a moment, then christened me with a new name. He said I reminded him of a wolf in that position, so he would call me "Guy White Wolf." I was honored. It's certainly better than "Little Weasel Trips and Falls."

The Peter Principle

The late Dr. Laurence J. Peter devoted his life to helping people avoid the principle that bears his name. I pass it along here because I consider it extremely important for those caught up in the illusions of success and climbing the corporate ladder.

The Peter Principle states that in a hierarchy individuals tend to rise to their level of incompetence. I'm certain the principle became famous because we've all seen this happen in the workplace. And if we're not careful, we can get trapped in it ourselves. Even Dr. Peter had to take extraordinary measures to keep from becoming a victim of his own principle.

Dr. Peter was offered a job as a department head at UCLA. He knew it was a job he did not want and would not do well, yet the administrators insisted that he take it. They held a top-level meeting for the express purpose of convincing him to accept the position that would mean a raise in pay and prestige.

Dr. Peter knew he would have to make a convincing argument that he was not the man for the job. So, while the administrators talked to him about the perks of the position, Dr. Peter walked over to a window, took out a magnifying glass, and tried to light a cigarette by focusing the sun's rays on it.

The job offer was rescinded.

Weep No More, My Mary

Mary Higgins Clark was a widow with five children when she decided to become a writer. She had no college education, and her only jobs had been as a secretary and airline attendant. With five kids, the only time she could find to write was from five until seven o'clock each morning—before the kids woke up.

Her first manuscript was rejected. So were her second, third, fourth, fifth, tenth, fifteenth, twentieth, thirtieth, and thirty-fifth. And then, after six years and forty rejections, she made her first sale—for $100.

Mary Higgins Clark later became the first writer in history to sign a publishing contract worth more than ten million dollars in guaranteed royalties. By then, she had a history of success with such best-sellers as: *Where Are The Children?*, *A Cry In The Night*, *The Cradle Will Fall*, and *Weep No More, My Lady*. And she also found time to get her college degree along the way.

The Monk

When I traveled to China in 1987, I interviewed a Buddhist monk. He lived in Jinan at the top of Thousand Buddha Mountain. Through an interpreter, I asked the monk where his peace and happiness came from, and I prepared to scribble his wisdom in my reporter's notebook. His answer has stayed with me ever since. He said, "It's been a very good tourist season, and I've made lots of money."

Qufu Graves

In Qufu, China, I visited the grave of Confucius. On some nearby graves I noticed some food. I learned that it is quite common for the Chinese to take food to the cemetery and leave it on the graves of their departed loved ones. Before you pass judgment on this practice, think for a minute. Who's going to smell the flowers you leave on the graves of *your* loved ones?

At the Great Wall of China working on a documentary of The Tucson Boys Chorus, 1987

A little "monky business" in Jinan

Tianenmen Square, 1987
The Chinese were afraid to speak to us about their government. Two years later,
when students spoke out in this same square, they were massacred.

A camel ride at the Great Wall

Standing on the hallowed ground of Masada in Israel, overlooking the Dead Sea, 1993

Planting a tree in Israel.

In Washington D.C. covering the Monica Lewinsky scandal, 1998

Visiting my friend Vic Fitzgaireld in Anchorage, Alaska, 2001

Victor Fitzgaireld, a man out standing in his field
He forgot his belt; hence the rope.

Tom Foley

Lonnie Campbell

Willie Cocio, also
known as Willie
Wise Eagle

At Old Tucson for a KGUN 9 promo shoot in 1985

Loitering at Le Buzz Cafe, my favorite coffee shop, where much of this book was written. My thanks to Dennis and Margaret Hadley for allowing me to use their establishment as my second office.

The warrior greeting sunrise at Aguas Blancas Beach in Ibiza

Three weeks living in a tent on a beautiful island with no phone, no fax, no computer. It was heaven.

Former Chicago TV personality Ellen Poulson helps coordinate my yoga classes and retreats. She's a godsend, but most of all—a good friend.

My daughter, Jami, enjoying the Oklahoma countryside.

My son, Neil, in the White Mountains.

My wife, Linda

Judging Jeffry

Jeffry Gallet was not your typical judge. Nobody expected him to do anything with his life. In fact, when his old friends heard that he was in court, they were surprised that he was a judge—and not the defendant. Gallet was never a good student. He graduated dead last in his high school class. He went on to law school and graduated dead last there, too.

It wasn't that he didn't try. He did. In fact, he would spend hours trying to read his assignments, but never quite managing to succeed. His classmates called him stupid. His teachers called him lazy.

Gallet never forgot the day in the seventh grade when he had turned in another failing paper. The teacher took that paper, marked on it a big, bright red "F" and then placed it on the bulletin board for everyone to see. The idea that he was a failure was hammered home in a way that would shatter anyone's self-esteem.

For Jeffry Gallet, the turning point came at the age of thirty-four when he went on a date with a psychologist. At the dinner table he did something that caught his dinner partner's attention. He moved his wine glass. The psychologist immediately asked, "Why did you move that glass?"

Gallet thought she was playing some kind of psychological game with him. But then she asked again, "Why did you move that glass?"

"I don't know," he replied. "I guess I tend to knock them over."

"I bet you don't know your left from your right."

"How did you know that?" he asked. "The only way I can remember which is left and which is right is by looking at my watch on my left wrist."

"I bet you can't spell either," she went on. Once again she was right. The psychologist insisted that he go in for testing. When he did, Jeffry Gallet found out that he had a learning disability. He found out he was *not* stupid, but he *was* different. And there were ways to cope.

Because of his struggles, Judge Gallet had a unique insight as to why so many juveniles wind up in court. Thirty-five percent of the children convicted of juvenile delinquency have undiagnosed learning disabilities. Next question: How do you earn a living if you can't read? Answers: crime or welfare. As the judge pointed out, crime has higher status in the community, and it pays more.

Right up until his untimely death in a traffic accident, Judge Gallet preached the gospel of perseverance. He always said: Find what you can do, and then do it. Don't dwell on your failures; focus on your successes. And above all, play to your strengths.

The judge certainly did that. He wrote numerous books—by dictation.

Nixon on the Day Kennedy Was Shot

One of the great interviewers of our time is Larry King of CNN. When he came to Phoenix for a speech at America West Arena several years ago, Larry and I spoke for several minutes, and he shared the following story.

LK: I was interviewing Nixon in 1967, he used to come down to Miami a lot and I knew him through his friend, B.B. Rebozo, and I got to be very friendly with Nixon. Five years after Kennedy was shot, I'm interviewing Nixon on TV in Miami, and just as an afterthought, I asked him, by the way, where were you when Kennedy was shot?

And he said, "You know no one's ever asked me. I left Dallas that day. I was with a law firm in New York and we represented Coca-Cola, and I was in Dallas representing them on legal matters. I was getting ready to fly back to New York, and as I was leaving Love Field they were preparing for the arrival of the president. A man sitting next to me said, 'You know for a couple thousand votes that could be you coming here today.' And I said I try not to think about it."

Nixon landed in New York and got off the plane. The driver who was supposed to meet him wasn't there. So Nixon got a cab and left the airport. Well, the cabdriver missed the turn onto Grand Central Parkway, so he had to go down a street and go back around to get onto Parkway. The cab stopped for a red light. It was the only car on the street, a little street in Queens near the airport. A door opened and a woman came running out of her house screaming.

Nixon rolled down his window and asked, "What's the matter?"

The woman saw Nixon and fainted. She had just heard Walter Cronkite say that Kennedy had been shot, then the first thing she saw was Richard Nixon, and she thought the world was coming to an end.

You Have to Give Her Credit

This story comes from Fritzi Carp-Ruiz who worked in the Hospice program at a Tucson geriatric center.

Fritzi remembers a ninety-year-old woman who was on the verge of death. It was just a matter of hours. The woman knew it and so did her family. The woman also knew she did not want to die in the geriatric center. She wanted to die at home in her own bed.

Fritzi realized that time was of the essence, so she called an ambulance. They put the woman into the ambulance, turned on the lights and siren, and headed for the woman's house. They carried her inside and gently helped her into the bed. But the woman was not quite through.

She asked for the telephone, her purse, and her favorite catalogue. Shopping had been her favorite pastime, and she thought—why not make the most of every minute?

The woman retrieved her credit card, placed a phone call, picked out a few things she wanted from the catalogue, and ordered them. Then she hung up, handed the credit card to her daughter, and said, "Here, you take care of it."

And then she died.

Hammering Home a Point

I never met Tom Campbell, but I know all about him from his granddaughter, news producer Heylie Eigen.

Tom was a cantankerous World War II veteran who lived to the age of seventy-four. He had lost a leg in the war, so he wore a wooden leg.

Once when Tom had to be rushed to the hospital for high blood pressure, he forgot his leg. His daughter, Donna Bishop, was given the job of retrieving the leg and taking it to him in the hospital. As she carried the leg through the corridors, people stared. Finally, she looked back at one person and said, "The rest of his parts are in the car."

But here's my favorite story about the wooden limb:

To amuse his young grandchildren, Tom occasionally would call them around, hand them a hammer, and let them pound nails into his wooden leg. Then he told them to go home and do the same thing to their father's legs.

It Says Volumes

In April of 1992, television did what it does best. It brought us live pictures of the riots in Los Angeles after the Rodney King verdict. Fifteen thousand people ran wild in the streets. By the time they were through, fifty-three people were dead, sections of L.A. were devastated, and officials put the damage at one billion dollars. What do I remember most? In the middle of the looting, hundreds of people were breaking into stores and running out with TVs, VCRs, and mattresses on their backs. But I'm going to remember what they *didn't* run out with. My mind goes back to that one shopping mall where every store had been ransacked except for one—the bookstore.

Many Distressing Disguises

When Mother Teresa came to Phoenix a few years before her death, a radio announcer asked how he could help others. The diminutive nun told him to look at the people on the street and to realize he was looking at Jesus in His many distressing disguises. The years did not change her message.

Some twenty years earlier I had covered Mother Teresa when she came to Miami, Florida to establish a home for abused women and children. It was amazing to see the number of people who traveled hundreds of miles just to be in her presence.

At a news conference, Mother Teresa preached to a crowd of reporters, and she said something I've never forgotten. She said, "I can see God in every human being."

If we could all say that—the news tonight at ten o'clock would be quite different.

Carlos

Just before this book went to print, Tucson lost one of its great-est leaders – a 16-year-old boy. Almost everyone knew Carlos Valencia, and many had tried to help him during his four-year struggle with leukemia. Carlos needed a bone-marrow trans-plant. We in the media put out the word, and Tucsonans re-sponded. Six-thousand tested to see if their marrow might be a match. The response resulted in a substantial increase in the national bone-marrow registry, and that, in turn, will increase the chances for other cancer patients to survive. But for Carlos, it was not to be.

On the day that Carlos slipped into a coma, reporter Deanne Donnelly quietly broke the news to me and others in the news-room. Deanne could hardly speak, and I felt the blood drain out of my face. I had to sit down. We all knew this could happen, but that didn't make it any easier. I had to request that Julie Myers read the initial story on the air because I simply could not. Later, once composed, I put together a tribute to Carlos.

I had interviewed Carlos several times, and like everyone who knew him, I became his friend. During one interview at his house, I asked Carlos why he always used the word "we" when referring to his personal struggle with cancer.

He replied, "When I say 'we' I'm talking about my mother and father and brother, all my relatives, all my friends, my doc-tors and nurses—and God. I'm not alone."

This was the bedrock for Carlos's faith. Regardless of what happened, Carlos knew in his heart that everything would be okay. Carlos was surrounded by love when he died on a Sunday night at University Medical Center.

Later that week, on the evening of Carlos's wake, monsoon rains dampened the streets around St. Augustine Cathedral. Reporter Sal Quijada noted: It was as if the heavens themselves were crying for Carlos.

Thousands of people attended the funeral mass. I'm sure many of them had never met Carlos or his family. They only knew the boy they had seen on TV, and they knew he was the real thing. At Holy Hope Cemetery I stood behind the Valencia family as hundreds of people filed past them to express their condolences. Many of the mourners were so overcome by grief they couldn't speak. I was one of the last in line.

I whispered to Carlos's mother, Cecilia, "Of all the people I've ever covered in the news..." That was all I could get out before choking up. But she knew what I meant. I'd never met anyone quite like Carlos.

Carlos's father, Ford, looked me in the eye and said compassionately, "Don't forget him."

How could I? How could anyone?

What Carlos stands for is what this book is all about–the ability to be greater than anything that can happen to you. The power to transcend what some might consider to be the end. To know it's really only the beginning. Despite his struggle, Carlos never lost his optimism, courage and faith. And this is his gift to us. *Para Carlos – Para Todos.*

For Carlos – For Us All.

We shall not cease from exploration, and the end of all our exploring will be to arrive where we started and know the place for the first time. —T. S. Eliot

Acknowledgements

I'm thankful to Linda Atchley for inspiring this book. It probably never would have been written without her. Thanks also to my son Neil Atchley for transcribing my interviews. And my appreciation goes to Dr. Tim Smith for his computer expertise and for being the first friend I made in Tucson almost twenty years ago.

I also wish to express my gratitude to KGUN 9, specifically general manager Ray Depa and news director Fernando Lopez, for allowing me to pursue my passion for positive news.

Les Is More

Organization has never been my strong point. For years many of the stories in this book languished in my laptop until Les Siemens and his lovely wife, Barb, helped me publish this book. They were the right people at the right time. Using their varied and immense talents, they brought the words and pictures to life. Les and Barb, thank you for helping my dream come true. Thank you for all the hard work. But, most of all, thank you for being the gentle, loving friends that you are.

About the Author

Guy Atchley is a reporter. For three decades he has chronicled the lives of ordinary people who have extraordinary determination. Their stories were featured in his television news series called "Guy Atchley's People" on KGUN 9 TV in Tucson, Arizona. Guy focuses on people whose stories motivate and inspire. And out of his own experiences Guy has developed his convictions about what it takes for a person to reach his or her potential.

Since he graduated from the University of Tulsa in 1972 with a Bachelor of Arts Degree in Radio/Television Speech, Guy has received more than twenty first-place awards for excellence in reporting. He has been in Tucson for twenty years now, and his KGUN 9 Newscast has been honored as Best Newscast seven times. In 1992 Guy swept the Arizona Associated Press Awards with three first-place honors including: Best Serious Feature, Best Light Feature, and Best General Reporting. Guy also was honored for his reports on living conditions in China in his documentary "China: 1987."

In October of 1993, Guy traveled to the Middle East for a documentary on Israel's quest for peace. That documentary plus Guy's news reports and community speeches to expose intolerance and bigotry earned him the 1994 Human Relations Award presented by the Jewish Community Relations Council.

In 1991, the Special Olympics Committee named Guy Arizona's Outstanding Broadcaster. The Rotary, Lions, Kiwanis, and Civitan Clubs also have honored Guy for his community service.

Guy has been the subject of news stories on ABC News, CBS News, CNN and in the *Wall Street Journal* as well as several other newspapers and magazines. He has appeared in three movies including the remake of *Vanishing Point, Runnin' at Midnite,* and *Jericho Fever.* In each film he played the role of a reporter.

Guy is thankful to be a real-life journalist. He has covered space shuttle launches in Florida, racial tension in the South, immigration policies at the U.S./Mexico border, journeys of healing to the Vietnam Veterans War Memorial in Washington, D.C., and the chaos of Capitol Hill during the Monica Lewinsky scandal.

Guy now balances his days by teaching yoga classes at Yoga Oasis East in Tucson. He also leads yoga retreats at such beautiful Southern Arizona locations as Holy Trinity Monastery in St. David and Club Kilimanjahro in Bisbee.

If you would like to:
- see behind the scenes at KGUN 9
- know about Guy's yoga classes and retreats
- inquire about Guy's speaking engagements

please visit his web site at www.guyatchley.com (http://www.guyatchley.com)

Index

214